Modern Drama: A Very Short Introduction

VERY SHORT INTRODUCTIONS are for anyone wanting a stimulating and accessible way into a new subject. They are written by experts, and have been translated into more than 40 different languages.

The series began in 1995, and now covers a wide variety of topics in every discipline. The VSI library now contains over 450 volumes—a Very Short Introduction to everything from Psychology and Philosophy of Science to American History and Relativity—and continues to grow in every subject area.

Very Short Introductions available now:

Available soon:

For more information visit our website

www.oup.com/vsi/

Kirsten E. Shepherd-Barr

MODERN DRAMA

A Very Short Introduction

OXFORD
UNIVERSITY PRESS

OXFORD

UNIVERSITY PRESS

Great Clarendon Street, Oxford, OX2 6DP,
United Kingdom

Oxford University Press is a department of the University of Oxford.
It furthers the University's objective of excellence in research, scholarship,
and education by publishing worldwide. Oxford is a registered trade mark of
Oxford University Press in the UK and in certain other countries

© Kirsten E. Shepherd-Barr 2016

The moral rights of the author have been asserted

First edition published in 2016

Impression: 1

Published in the United States of America by Oxford University Press
198 Madison Avenue, New York, NY 10016, United States of America

British Library Cataloguing in Publication Data

Data available

Library of Congress Control Number: 2015952189

ISBN 978-0-19-965877-0

Printed in Great Britain by
Ashford Colour Press Ltd, Gosport, Hampshire

Contents

List of illustrations

Introduction

Modern drama is often characterized by alienation and hostility, whether it's between the actors and their audiences, the playwright and the actors, or the playwright and the audience. Plays signal this sense of opposition in their titles (as in Peter Handke's *Offending the Audience*), as do studies of modern drama (recent books include *Against Theatre*, *Performing Opposition*, *Antitheatricality*, *Unmaking Mimesis*, and *The Death of Character*). Even the phrase commonly used to describe metatheatre—'breaking the fourth wall'—has the ring of violence and disruption to it, when metatheatre in fact simply means 'a play within a play', or the kind of theatre that draws attention to, rather than trying to hide, the fact that what you are watching is merely the illusion of reality.

This book takes as its starting point a sense of opposition, breaking with convention, and moving into a new relationship with the audience to explore modern drama and the changing nature of theatrical experience. It looks at how playwrights, directors, actors, and designers question, pull apart, even attack the very medium in which they are working, in order to reassemble and refashion it; what Martin Puchner and Alan Ackerman refer to as a fundamental antitheatricality underpinning modern drama and causing its 'creative destructions'. And this dynamic also includes the audience, which is just as much under siege as the event it is watching.

1

Modern drama's disruption and hostility are part of the modernist transgression of boundaries in all the arts, for instance in the angular abstractions of cubist painting, in poetry that abandons traditional form, metre, and verse, in novels that experiment with free-flowing 'stream of consciousness' narration, or in the unmelodic atonal dissonance of music by Bartok or Schoenberg.

Theatre similarly rejected tradition, not gradually but through a series of brief but powerful theatrical explosions that began in the final decades of the 19th century. From the outrage over Ibsen's *Ghosts* and the riots that accompanied *Ubu Roi* and *The Playboy of the Western World*, to the discomfort of audiences at the premieres of *Waiting for Godot* and *Look Back in Anger*, to the near-universal disgust at Sarah Kane's *Blasted*, the story of modern drama is a tale of extremes, testing both audiences and actors to their limits. The unifying thread throughout this narrative is this new note of hostility: modern dramatists, directors, and actors start to drive a wedge between themselves and the audience, prising apart the relatively cosy relationship that had come to dominate the stage over the preceding centuries.

This book tells the story of modern drama through its seminal, groundbreaking plays and performances and the sheer artistic diversity that these represent. Spanning a period from roughly 1880 to the present, it covers the major developments of modern drama two decades per chapter, from early modernist theatre in the 1880s through post-war developments to the present day. These demarcations are meant as general guidelines, as nothing fits perfectly within rigid time frames: Brecht's career spans many decades and his influence continues to this day; Beckett can be considered both modernist and postmodernist. Within each chapter, a range of plays will be discussed coming mainly from Europe and America. Although a full consideration of non-Western drama lies beyond the scope of this study, I discuss important developments outside these geographical boundaries that have played a significant role in the history of modern drama and shaped the way plays are written and performed.

I use the term 'drama' in its fullest sense, emphasizing the dual nature of the drama as both text and performance. Modern drama has been transformed by the emergence of the director, a presence we now take utterly for granted in the theatre yet one that didn't exist until the late 19th century. Productions of certain plays under a particular director have often exerted a powerful impact: think of *Ubu Roi*, *Ghosts*, *The Fairground Booth*, *Look Back in Anger*, *Marat/Sade*, or *Angels in America*. This book charts the director's rise to prominence through specific examples like Antoine, Lugné-Poe, Reinhardt, Appia, Craig, Artaud, Brecht, Cocteau, Meyerhold, and on to more contemporary practitioners such as Katie Mitchell and Simon McBurney.

Another key element to modern drama is the emergence of new theories to explain it. Individual plays and productions changed the way people thought about the theatre in the 20th century, but so too did a growing body of theoretical writing by the practitioners themselves, describing and reflecting on their work. From Zola and Stanislavski to Artaud and Brecht to Schechner and Grotowski, theories of the theatre have come to play an increasingly important role over the last 120 years—alongside the legitimizing of drama and theatre arts, playwriting, and performance studies as academic subjects within institutions of higher education—and have continued to exercise a profound influence.

Drama is like palaeontology: we study the fossils (play texts) that remain after the full dramatic experience (the performance) has died. 'The evidence has forever receded from the thing itself', writes theatre scholar Joseph Roach, and we are 'extrapolating from the position of a few old bones', studying a fossil record that 'keeps most of the secrets of its incompletion'. While this book will rely mostly on those bones—the texts of plays—it will put flesh on them wherever possible by allusion to performance contexts, with the aim of giving the fullest possible meaning to these works as living 'drama'.

Plays are the end result of a complex web of forces, and the changes in the way plays were written in the late 19th century go hand in hand with changes in the conditions of performance and staging. The introduction of electricity into theatres around 1880 is one example of this: the change that it ushered in from gaslight to electric lighting radically altered the way plays were performed, what actors could portray (more subtle emotion), how to control an audience by plunging it into darkness, and made acting safer for the actors by reducing the risk of fire. It also created the 'fourth wall', whereby the stage is a room with the fourth wall removed (or rather, the audience *is* the fourth wall, silent, unacknowledged, eavesdropping). This in turn affected the writing of plays, with more psychologically developed characters and domestic interiors revealing the inevitable skeletons in the closet.

A play like Ibsen's *Ghosts* (1881) is the end result of all of these kinds of changes acting together, simultaneously enabling and created by more realistic acting, scenery, and lighting. Another example of how contingent plays are, how dependent on their generative theatrical circumstances, is the famous tarantella scene of Ibsen's *A Doll's House* (1879). This moment when Nora dances almost out of control is seen as a vital episode in the play, wordlessly conveying Nora's psychological state and signalling the unbearable societal pressures on women. Yet Ibsen apparently put it in the play because the actress who was playing Nora for its first production anywhere in Europe happened to be particularly skilful in dancing the tarantella.

Luck, opportunism, serendipity, expediency, practicality—call it what you want, it's a key component of drama and a reminder that some of the most enduring qualities of plays considered 'classic' today had nothing to do with the text (or indeed the playwright). Modern drama gives us powerful, indelible images: two tramps beneath a bare tree, a woman up to her neck in a pile of earth, a peasant woman dragging a cart of goods. It has also given us new words, like 'Pinteresque'. One of the best examples of this serendipity comes from a play called *R.U.R.* written by two Czech brothers, Josef and Karel Čapek, in 1923, warning about dangers of an increasing reliance on mechanization for the workers of tomorrow. Though few people read or see the play nowadays, it has left a powerful legacy through its coining of a single word that is now universally used: 'robot'.

Chapter 1
Realism, naturalism, and symbolism

The two decades from 1880–1900 are astonishing not just for the new ideas about drama and the radical changes in theatre practice and playwriting, but for the pace of those developments. More changes and upheavals are packed into these twenty years than perhaps any other period of modern drama.

Very few people originally saw some of the plays we now consider worth studying, like Shaw's *Widowers' Houses*, which exposed the problem of slum landlords in London. In 1892, the play was given its premiere by the Independent Theatre (formed in part to get around stage censorship) before a tiny audience. In the same year *Charley's Aunt*, an entertaining romp that hardly anyone now reads or sees, enjoyed a run of nearly 1,500 performances. To put this in perspective, one hundred performances is about the length of a respectable run. In a short introduction to modern drama, it is impossible to give equal attention to both kinds of plays, and such histories tend to favour the progressive and subversive over the popular and 'merely' entertaining. But it is worth bearing in mind that for each play under discussion, there were dozens of plays like *Charley's Aunt*.

One of the unique features of modern drama is that some of the key performances took place in inauspicious or ephemeral circumstances; 'great reckonings in small rooms', as director and scholar Herbert Blau reminds us, that have taken on canonical status. Playwright and actress Elizabeth Robins recalled seeing the 'poverty-struck' premiere of *A Doll's House* in London in 1889 with its little-known actors in a 'pokey, dingy theatre' and 'sparse, rather dingy audience'. For her, this made it 'less like a play than like a personal meeting—with people and issues that seized us and held us, and wouldn't let us go'. It is a paradox of theatre history that many of the plays we now regard as pioneering were at first fleeting and precarious affairs, and that in many cases performance *precedes* text.

Yet even as this new style of playwriting and production that Robins is describing—realism—was taking hold, many playwrights were seeking ways of staving off the inevitable passivity that an invisible audience would fall prey to, sitting quietly in the dark and watching events unfold. Laurence Senelick writes that because of censorship across Europe and the 'self-protective nature of theatre managements, the stage, as was its mandate, tended to endorse community values and reinforce the audience in its prejudices'. Modern drama emerges through its attempts to shock the bourgeoisie, to provoke and outrage it, to prod it out of that passive and self-contented state. Yet the 'spectator as stooge' motif had to be constantly renegotiated, as bourgeois audiences became hip to the attacks playwrights levied at them and, deftly absorbing each new shock, could very quickly grow bored.

Precedents

There were in fact earlier works for the stage well before this period that signal a startlingly modern theatricality yet don't fit into a too-neat timeline of modern drama that would have it start in 1880. One such example is Georg Büchner's *Woyzeck* (1837). This unfinished fragment of a play, later to inspire the opera by Alban Berg, concerns a man driven to murdering his wife partly through jealousy and partly through his extreme psychological state brought about by being the subject of a mad doctor's experiment in which he can only eat peas. The episodic nature of the play—consisting of discrete episodes rather than causally connected, organically linked scenes—as well as its naturalistic qualities of character and setting (suggesting the struggle between humans and their environment as well as their often ungovernable and violent impulses) are often invoked as proto-modernist; the play seems sixty years ahead of its time. Similarly, Henrik Ibsen's *Peer Gynt* (1867) seems presciently modern with its episodic structure and vivid anti-hero searching for (and shirking) the concept of selfhood. 'Be thyself—enough!' proclaim the trolls who lure Peer into their subterranean world, and the rest of the play charts his adventures as he tries to come to terms with what it means to be oneself fully.

Peer Gynt is written in verse, as were so many plays of the period. But in the 1870s Ibsen permanently changed the nature of drama by renouncing poetry in favour of prose. He felt that writing in verse was out of sync with a modern literature that 'submitted problems to debate', as the influential Danish literary critic Georg Brandes put it. Ibsen went against the idealism then dominating art and announced that what inspired him was 'the opposite...the dregs and sediment of one's own nature' (what Yeats would call 'the foul rag-and-bone shop of the heart'). Modern playwrights have followed suit, challenging or entirely reconfiguring the idea of the hero or heroine, blurring neat distinctions between good and bad and suggesting that ordinary people contain the stuff of heroism and, conversely, that the aristocrat is no more worthy of representation than the butcher.

Ibsen and the drama of everyday life

To convey 'the dregs and sediment' of human nature, Ibsen turned not just to prose but the prosaic, the ordinary. From *The Pillars of Society* (1877) onwards he used everyday language to create dialogue that sounds ordinary but contains deep psychological nuances. Characters hesitate, interrupt one another, fail to finish their thoughts, and rarely use long speeches or soliloquies, but they are profound and fully fleshed out in ways that belie the superficial simplicity of their language. 'Mrs Alving, you are a very guilty mother', says Pastor Manders in Act I of *Ghosts*. After a silence, she replies ('slowly, and with control', according to the stage directions):

> MRS ALVING: You have had your say, Pastor Manders. And tomorrow you will make a speech in my husband's memory. I shall not speak tomorrow. But now I'm going to talk to you just as you have talked to me.
> MANDERS: Of course, you want to make excuses for what you did ...
> MRS ALVING: No. I just want to tell you something.
> MANDERS: Well?

She proceeds to tell him that he knows nothing about what really happened to her in the past, that he abandoned her to her miserable marriage instead of helping her as he could have done, that he—a man of the cloth—is a coward and a hypocrite.

This is a central moment, rendered in deceptively simple language: Mrs Alving is finding her voice, speaking her mind, right in front of the audience. The stripped-back quality of such dialogue shone through in the 2013 production of *Ghosts* directed by Stephen Unwin that toured England (and that brilliantly recreated the sets designed by Edvard Munch for a 1906 production of the play by Max Reinhardt), in a version that underscored how this speech is one of many in the play that show Mrs Alving searching for a voice as she repeatedly insists 'let me speak...I want to say...', all the while surrounded by forceful male figures who threaten to drown her out.

And the language fits the situation. Ibsen depicted domestic interactions and social problems that every audience recognized: shallow, unhappy marriages; unfulfilled wives; financial struggles and bankruptcy; pollution and ecological damage due to modern industry; political corruption and cover-up. But he gave these everyday settings and characters depth and context, and in so doing challenged assumptions about right and wrong. In *A Doll's House* (1879), Nora discusses her secrets with Mrs Linde, telling her how she had to forge her dying father's signature to borrow the money needed to take her husband to Italy for his health, a trip that saved his life. She sees nothing wrong with her forgery since it had a happy outcome and harmed no one. And we have to take her word for it. All this has happened years before the play begins; Ibsen picks up where most dramatists would have ended, focusing on the *aftermath* of events rather than the events themselves, and the audience needs to pay close attention to this complex exposition scene and reconstruct the past as bits of it are gradually revealed. A woman at thirty is much more interesting than her newlywed self, Ibsen seems to be saying, and likewise plays that end with marriage are much less interesting than plays that show what happens after it.

Yet far from being an exercise in objective realism, there is a theatrical and performative undertone to *A Doll's House* (whose title in English translation hardly captures the pointed strangeness of the original Dano-Norwegian 'et dukkehjem', which translates as 'a doll home'; where, Ibsen asks, are women 'at home' in a world of double standards?). The play suggests that identity is an artificial construct: we watch Nora watching herself acting, creating (and recreating) a role for herself. If it can be created, it can also be destroyed and made anew, with better ingredients. This is another reason why those dramatic events are not shown but recounted by Nora; the audience sees them through *her* eyes, constructs action and character through *her* verbal cues. The play riffs on this idea of performance of self, and by the end gender roles are reversed: in their final discussion scene Nora speaks calmly and 'imperturbably' while Torvald 'jumps up' and 'struggles to keep his composure'. She takes control and acts decisively, he breaks down, pleads, and nearly becomes hysterical. In a series of brief but devastating exchanges (Torvald: 'No man sacrifices his honour for the one he loves'. Nora: 'Millions of women have done so') Ibsen gives us only, in Emile Zola's term, 'strictly useful words'.

Naturalism in the theatre

Zola insisted that modern theatre should take its inspiration from the increasingly scientific context of late 19th-century Europe. Darwin's *On the Origin of Species* (1859) and, especially, *The Descent of Man* (1871) opened up new possibilities for art to explore the relationship of humans to their environment as well as to each other. How far are we shaped by our environment (which we can usually do something about), and how far is it heredity that determines who we are (and which we can't do anything about)? Today we would call this debate 'nature versus nurture'.

Zola urged dramatists to foreground this scientific thinking in their plays. 'Nothing is stable in society,' he wrote, 'everything is carried along by sustained motion.' Darwinian natural selection showed that species change over time rather than remaining fixed, and this in turn called into question the notion of an overall design or plan in nature. No one was directing nature's development; it was all down to randomness and blind chance. The one thing that was certain was that things changed; and this essential quality of life is also at the heart of most dramas, which reveal the processes of change in people's circumstances, stories, and character. Zola wanted to see people of 'flesh and bones on the stage ... scientifically analyzed'. He aligned himself with 'anatomists, analysts ... [and] compilers of human data'.

Some playwrights, although attracted to this idea, were uneasy about the implication that theatre was merely a vehicle for a scientifically exact rendering of life. Strindberg—whose career, like Ibsen's, went through several distinct phases and who was himself deeply attracted to science—hailed Zola's words and produced *Miss Julie* (1888), proclaiming a new kind of drama that distinguished between the kind of 'misunderstood naturalism' that 'photographs everything but actually reveals nothing' and the 'great naturalism' that depicts the 'great battles' and delights in the conflict between powerful human forces. Above all, he urged dramatists to view reality subjectively, rather than attempt neutrally to reflect it; for instance, *Miss Julie*'s exploration of the inescapable forces that shape and drive us, and the pressures of the environment on the individual, are strongly informed by a misogyny that attributes Julie's erring behaviour to her mother's feminism, as a result of which Julie is 'half woman, half man'.

Miss Julie shows the devastating outcome of sexual attraction between the aristocratic Julie and her servant Jean. Their sexual encounter is not shown, of course—that would not be feasible on the stage—but occurs offstage during a dance held by the peasants on the estate. We see the dance, and we can imagine what is going on in the next room. When the couple re-emerges, Jean denounces his conquest and punctures her desperate dream of their escape to start a new life elsewhere: 'Menial's whore, lackey's harlot, shut your mouth and get out of here! Are you the one to lecture me for being coarse?' he says to her. Seeing that he does not care for her, and knowing that there is no future for her now that she has 'fallen' both sexually and in terms of class, Julie commits suicide.

Fallen women were everywhere in plays and in fiction, truly a 19th-century type, and they invariably committed suicide, met with some fatal accident, or died of disease, restoring moral order to the world they had disrupted while briefly titillating audiences with their overt sexuality. *Miss Julie* follows this pattern; so does Henry Arthur Jones's *The Case of Rebellious Susan* (1894) and Arthur Wing Pinero's *The Second Mrs Tanqueray* (1893), which caused a sensation for its sympathetic treatment of the fallen woman, portrayed by the leading actress, Mrs Patrick Campell. The difference between this play and Wilde's contemporaneous *A Woman of No Importance* is illuminating: both feature fallen women, yet where Paula Tanqueray dies of shame, Wilde's Mrs Arbuthnot defiantly declares that it was worth it—if she had to do it all again she would. 'Child of my shame, be still the child of my shame!' Far from dying, by the end of the play she dismisses her seducer as 'a man of no importance'.

Old forms, new voices

The plays I have discussed so far as examples of the new realism actually contain elements of two important 19th-century theatrical forms: melodrama and the well-made play. Melodramas involved stock characters such as the young ingénue, the hero, the villain, and a great deal of suspense as well as breathtaking stage scenery that included full-scale train crashes, waterfalls, burning forests, and watery caves. In the early 1850s, stage versions of *Uncle Tom's Cabin* sensationally depicted Eva's escape across the ice floes pursued by Legree and his yapping hounds.

But as entertaining as these melodramatic spectacles were, audiences wanted more substance. Already in the 1860s, T.W. Robertson in England introduced greater realism on stage through his 'cup and saucer' domestic dramas. Characters conversed in natural language and discussed familiar topics like marriage and courtship. Even scenes set in foreign lands, as in the Crimean War hut setting of *Ours* (1866), were domesticated: a wooing young couple makes a roly-poly pudding on stage, turning the exotic into the cosily English. Although the characters are not psychologically well developed and the plays can verge on sentimentality, Robertson brought natural, everyday dialogue to his dramas. But the course he seemed to be carving out for the theatre was diverted by the overwhelming popularity of the well-made play, a French import whose key exponents were Sardou, Dumas fils, and Scribe.

The *pièce bien faite*, which came to dominate European theatre in the latter half of the 19th century, involved a complicated plot, recognizable character types, a plethora of items (jewellery, handkerchiefs, letters) discovered at key moments leading to identities revealed, risqué situations, and fallen women (think of the high-class courtesan in *La Dame aux Camélias*). Wilde's society dramas consistently send up such devices ('What is this?' cries Mabel Chiltern in *An Ideal Husband*, 'Someone has dropped a diamond brooch!') as well as challenging the condemnation of the fallen woman. The well-made play typically followed a trajectory of *exposition*, *climax*, and *dénouement* (a satisfying resolution wrapping up the final scenes of exciting action). This is what Zola contemptuously dismissed as the 'theatre of fabrication', which he hoped to be replaced one day by a 'stage of observation'. Although the term 'well-made' sounds like it should be a compliment, it is in fact quite the opposite.

Ibsen recrafted this type of drama so that rather than ending with a climax and resolution, his plays ended with a discussion scene that analysed the problem that the play had laid bare but did not resolve it. As the curtain comes down on *Ghosts*, an agonized Mrs Alving stands undecided as to whether to administer the fatal dose of morphine to her son; the burden is on the audience to imagine what she does next. At the end of *A Doll's House*, Nora simply walks out, presumably for good, and there is no indication of what she would—or indeed *could*—do next, since as she has just explained she has no proper education, no skills, and no money; how could she even do the one acceptable job for a genteel woman at the time (governess)? Stage and prose sequels proliferated, including one by Shaw, imagining what happened to Nora after the curtain had come down, and at least one German production changed the ending so that Nora sank to the floor at Torvald's feet in abject recognition that if she left she would be failing in her duties as a mother (a scene Ibsen himself had to provide, due to inadequate copyright protection for dramatic authors at the time).

In short, Ibsen's plays showed the kinds of people and problems that his bourgeois audiences recognized as their own. One critic at the time imagined married couples going home after *A Doll's House* sitting silently at opposite sides of their carriages, in shock at seeing a play that mirrored—and dissected—their own unsatisfactory relationships. Ibsen's characters collapsed the distinctions between good and bad that had helped to define melodrama. Krogstad and Torvald are both sympathetic in their own ways, and they too learn truths about themselves and their socially conditioned expectations. Ibsen shows that we are all victims of societal conventions and false ideals. Yet he was equally capable of questioning his own zeal to expose the lies at the foundation of social structures. In *The Wild Duck* (1884), the truth about a couple's relationship, and a girl's true parentage, is revealed, but only to the despair of the child, who commits suicide. The play asks: what good did the revelation of truth do? People need their sustaining life-lies.

Comic relief

Oscar Wilde's theatre, transmuting Ibsen's ideas to the modes of comedy and farce, likewise champions the lie, the mask, the innocuous deception, as in the 'bunburying' of *The Importance of Being Earnest* (1895). He skewers bourgeois notions of earnestness, good conduct, and morality. A man's name matters more to his future wife than his character, and that name must be Ernest or nothing. A young woman fabricates her engagement to a man she has just met, producing letters, diary entries, and an engagement ring to prove their courtship. The warm friendship that two young women profess for each other when they have only just met turns in an instant to animosity when they discover (erroneously, it turns out) that they are rivals for the same man. An aristocratic and imposing mother sizes her future son-in-law up: 'Do you smoke?' 'Well, yes, I must admit I smoke.' 'I am glad to hear it. A man should always have an occupation of some kind. There are far too many idle men in London as it is.'

George Bernard Shaw admired Wilde's verbal fireworks, and made wit one of his own dramatic weapons, the sugar that coats his bitter pills. He began as a music and theatre critic but, on encountering Ibsen's works, turned his hand to playwriting in the mid-1890s, launching a career that spanned over five decades, producing dozens of original plays, and bringing lasting innovations to theatrical practice (see the discussion of the Court Theatre in Chapter 2). His *Mrs Warren's Profession* (1893), which depicts prostitution as if it were just like any other job, was banned by the Lord Chamberlain and had to wait until 1925 for its first public performance in London (see Box 1).

Box 1 Censorship

Theatrical censorship in Britain lasted from 1737 till 1968. Playwrights had to submit their scripts to the Lord Chamberlain, who would then decide whether the play should be granted a licence for performance. Very often he would require changes to the script before it could be performed, usually removing political, sexual, or otherwise morally suspect material. Sometimes he would refuse to license a play, as in the case of Ibsen's *Ghosts* (1881) and Shaw's *Mrs Warren's Profession* (1893).

Shaw protested, like so many others, against theatrical censorship and got around it by working with independent theatre companies, staging new European dramas as well as his own plays in private venues and by subscription. Others, like Wilde, ingeniously evaded censorship by burying their sharp social criticism beneath a shimmering surface wit and seemingly innocuous situations that seemed to follow the formula of the well-made play while subtly undermining it.

Wilde's epigrams, hinging on deliciously witty paradox—such as 'Nothing succeeds like excess'—disarmed audiences and disguised his exposure of hypocrisy and skewering of Puritanical values such as duty and virtue. Wilde shows that comedy could just as effectively 'submit problems to debate' as serious drama. Clotilde Graves' hit play *A Mother of Three* (1896) likewise uses farce to suggest that women can successfully take on men's roles in life as well as on the stage. The play's 'sustained jocularity' had the audience laughing 'pretty continuously', wrote Shaw in his review.

Shaw (like Wilde) was especially taken with Ibsen's liberating dramatic treatment of women. 'There is one law for men and another for women', wrote Ibsen in his prefatory notes to *A Doll's House*, a play that he dubbed 'the modern tragedy'. A critic noted that *Ghosts* was 'essentially a woman's play, a woman's story addressed to women'.

Ibsen's choice to focus on a female as the main character of the drama is part of his revolutionary approach to playwriting. From Nora and Mrs Alving, to Ellida in *The Lady from the Sea* and Hedda and Thea in *Hedda Gabler*, to the precocious Hilde Wangel of *The Master Builder*, to the sex-starved Rita Allmers in *Little Eyolf* and beyond, Ibsen plumbed the female condition and increasingly challenged what was acceptable feminine behaviour on stage. He was one of the first dramatists to recognize the plight of women as the stuff of modern drama, as a key element of what theatre scholar John Gassner called the 'mental climate' of plays. The New Woman, a term first used in 1894, rapidly took hold in the theatre. While some playwrights satirized her, others mined the new possibilities for character and situation that she opened up.

Shock, controversy, and retreat

One of these was the American actress, playwright, and novelist Elizabeth Robins who worked in London during the 1890s and appeared in some of the first performances of Ibsen's plays, at one point forming her own theatre company with the actress Marion Lea in order to put them on.

In 1893 Robins and her close friend Florence Bell anonymously adapted a Swedish short story for the stage that they called *Alan's Wife*. The play showed a woman killing her disfigured infant in an act that she refuses to explain, adopting silence throughout her trial and leaving everyone, including the audience, guessing: was it euthanasia? Was it an extreme, distorted manifestation of maternal love? Was it post-partum depression, or grief at her husband's death shortly before the child was born? Infanticide had been seen on the London stage, but not with such disturbing ambivalence. Likewise, the Finnish playwright Minna Canth's *Anna Liisa* (1895) scandalized audiences in Helsinki with its sympathetic heroine who had killed her child and was haunted by the act. Only Tolstoy's five-act tragedy *The Power of Darkness* (1886) has a more harrowing depiction of baby-killing.

From infanticide to syphilis (depicted in Ibsen's *Ghosts*, and in Brieux's *Damaged Goods*), from breastfeeding to prostitution and suicide and women rebelling against their narrowly prescribed roles, drama was beginning to show more and more controversial subject matter.

Yet arguably none of this would have been possible without the simultaneous revolutions that occurred in all areas of theatre—stagecraft, acting, publishing, and so on—which contributed to the new kind of drama being written. Without the flexibility created by electric lighting (replacing the dangerous gaslight still in use), without the introduction of the box set and more sophisticated scenery and stage design, and without new copyright laws to protect dramatic authors (such as the 1887 Berne Convention), the more subtle and deep dialogue Ibsen, Robins, Strindberg, Shaw, and others were pioneering could not have been heard, and the psychological nuances of character would have been lost.

The way these developments are intertwined can be seen in the integration of staging into the texts of plays, with stage directions describing interiors in detail as well as giving insight into character. André Antoine, director of the Théâtre Libre in Paris, which premiered several of Ibsen's plays and spearheaded theatrical naturalism, took radical steps like turning his back on the audience and speaking in a whisper. He could only do this because the audience was 'invisible', quiet, listening in the dark due to the new use of electric lighting. We take them for granted now, but such moves infuriated conservative critics like Francisque Sarcey. In other words, dramatic innovation and technological advances go hand in hand.

How groups behave on stage also came under radical rethinking and became a key element of the new theatrical realism. 'There are no small parts, only small actors'—the mantra often quoted to aspiring actors—originates in such practices as the German-based Meiningen Court theatre troupe's giving 'character' to each actor's role, no matter how insignificant, and making crowds dynamic rather than static and superficial. Yet even as these developments were changing the very nature of the theatrical experience, in some quarters there was increasing dissatisfaction with the mundaneness and banality of realistic topics and settings. Frustrated by the materiality of the stage and the physical reality of the actor's body, theatre was already starting off in new directions, such as symbolism and avant-garde experiments that attempted to make plays more suggestive, abstract, and metaphysical—less grounded in real and tangible everyday life.

What Yeats called the 'Savage God' found theatrical expression in the play *Ubu Roi* (1896) by Alfred Jarry, which caused a scandal for its subject matter, its staging, and its scatological language (the first word of the play is 'Merdre!'—an obvious allusion to 'merde', or 'shit'). The play was a pastiche of *Macbeth* and Jarry's schoolboy writings depicting one of his teachers as an obese, bumbling tyrant with a target painted on his belly and a toilet brush for a sceptre (Figure 1). Jarry had his artist friends, an avant-garde group called the Nabis that included Sérusier, Vuillard, and

1. 'Merdre!' Alfred Jarry's woodcut of his cartoonish and scatological King Ubu, wielding a toilet brush in place of a sceptre; for his 1896 play *Ubu Roi* at the Théâtre de l'Œuvre, Paris.

Toulouse-Lautrec, paint a continuous backdrop that incongruously juxtaposed (in Jarry's words) 'doors opening onto snow-covered plains under blue skies, mantelpieces with clocks on them swinging open to turn into doorways, and palm trees flourishing at the foot of beds so that little elephants perching on bookshelves can graze on them'.

Ubu Roi made a mockery of both realistic theatre and Wagner's concept of a 'total' theatre, the ideal of a synthesis of all the ingredients of drama and performance (music, text, scenery, lighting) into a *Gesamtkunstwerk*. And it was produced in the same theatre in Paris that gave birth to symbolist drama, which is based on this concept. Wagner's lasting legacy for drama is the emphasis on theatricality. But it is in the reaction against 'total art' that theatre truly innovates—when it begins to distrust this harmonious aesthetic as just as 'fake' as realism. Theatre historians Alan Ackerman and Martin Puchner suggest that modern drama's constant oscillation between 'the concrete detail of realism and a poetics of abstraction' is one of its most constructive qualities. They argue that modern drama is characterized by a creative destructiveness, theatrical forms and conventions destroyed in order to be remade, even—in the case of avant-garde theatre—capable of attacking and annihilating itself.

Belgian playwright Maurice Maeterlinck developed symbolist theatre in the 1890s in an effort to slough off the naturalistic chains binding the drama to the prosaic, material, and corporeal realities of everyday life at the expense of the abstract, metaphysical, and poetic dimensions. He found his inspiration not just in symbolist poets like Baudelaire and Mallarmé but in Ibsen's late plays from *The Master Builder* (1892) through *When We Dead Awaken* (1900), with their 'dialogue of the second degree'—underneath the very ordinary speech in which characters are speaking, they are carrying on another dialogue communicating their inner selves.

Maeterlinck's *The Intruder* and *The Blind* emulate these models but go even further in their rejection of realism in favour of abstraction and mystery, creating a theatre of stasis. Characters simply wait in the darkness, listening to the sounds of leaves rustling in the wind, talking of some mysterious event that is expected to happen yet never does. There is a direct line between these plays and the theatrical work of Samuel Beckett in the late 20th century.

Tragic-comedy as the modern mode

Modern drama breaks down distinct categories such as the tragic and the comic, and Russian playwright Anton Chekhov was one of the pioneers in this regard. Plays like *The Seagull* (which parodies symbolist drama) and *Uncle Vanya*, written in the late 1890s, blur the line between comedy and tragedy and challenge the basic stuff of drama, replacing action for the most part with talk. 'My dear, don't leave me alone with Vanya,' Serebryakov implores his wife, 'he'll talk my head off.'

Chekhov reintroduces the monologue into the drama and reinvents it, packing in even more 'talk' in this way but not necessarily 'saying' anything obviously revelatory with these long speeches. Because his characters talk so much but do little and can seem languid and enervated, he was called the 'dramatist of inaction'—though beside Maeterlinck's static dramas Chekhov's positively teem with incident. The hints of deep inner conflicts and emotions, desires, and passions are all there in Chekhov's dialogue, as the Russian actor and director Constantin Stanislavski showed in his staging of Chekhov's plays at the newly formed Moscow Art Theatre, beginning with *The Seagull* in 1898 and inaugurating a revolution in acting that permanently changed how actors prepare their roles. His organic, holistic system involves the whole body and mind of the actor, tapping his/her own emotions and histories for subtext, drawing on 'emotion memory' and the 'magic if' (imagining oneself *as* the character, not adopting an existing 'type').

The period 1880–1900 thus culminates in the launch of a powerful new method that would come to dominate acting and the theatre even while strong reactions to it were brewing and were about to generate some of the stage's most 'creative destructions'.

Questioning realism

It is easy to forget how revolutionary the new realistic drama was at the time. 'Naturalism and realism were the first dramatic modes to consider themselves not as expressions of the dominant political and ideological order,' writes theatre scholar W.B. Worthen, 'but as criticizing the values and institutions of middle-class society.' The problem is that nothing can be *changed* by a realistic representation; even if it is critical of modern society, 'realistic drama tacitly accepts the world and its values as an unchanging, and unchangeable, environment in which the characters live out their lives'. This is directly opposed to the dynamics of change suggested by Zola's embrace of Darwin, as discussed earlier in this chapter.

Not surprisingly, a reaction against realism begins in the 1890s and the desire to 'unmake mimesis', as theatre scholar Elin Diamond so aptly puts it, becomes the driving force of much subsequent drama, right through to the present day. The concept of 'realism' is inherently impossible and problematic. How do you represent everyone's reality? It will be different if you are black, female, non-European, and so on. Theatre cannot work like a mirror held up to nature, because there will always be someone holding that mirror, directing its point of view, and choosing which part of life it should reflect.

The striking thing about these two decades—the thing that makes this period of drama unique—is that so many radically different, and often directly opposite, tendencies were being explored. Theatre encompassed so many modes; this is what makes it problematic to try to define and characterize what is happening in 'theatre' as a unified, coherent whole. Yet there are some common features running through all these different threads: experiment, innovation, and language. Widening the horizon of theatre, and its audience's expectations, through new forms and ideas lies at the heart of many of these seemingly competing developments (realism, symbolism). Likewise, the desire to make theatre, as critic John Gassner put it, 'rich in language' is a unifying motive.

At the same time, one cannot understate the importance of the material side—how the visual and physical dimensions of theatre in this period were drastically changing. Technological developments meant that to go to the theatre and to see a play was never the same again. These caused the spectrum of theatrical presentation and styles to widen considerably, enabling both modest, fleeting, yet groundbreaking performances like *Alan's Wife* and, at the other extreme, the founding of national theatres across Europe—spaces of spectacular scale and opulence. Theatre was arguably at the peak of its dominance as a cultural form—even as, already towards the end of the century, the rise of cinema, the cheap novel, and the proliferation of competing entertainments would threaten to push it to the margins of culture.

Chapter 2
Sex, suffrage, and scandal

The century begins with an ending: Ibsen's final play, *When We Dead Awaken* (1900). This abstract, brooding work was applauded by the young James Joyce, himself an aspiring playwright whose play *Exiles* was published in 1916 and loosely resembles the triangular love story of *When We Dead Awaken*. Both plays are meditations on what it means to be an artist and, specifically, what theatre means in a modern context, once realism has become so firmly established as the dominant, and perhaps stifling, mode.

This chapter gives a sense of the turbulence and experimentation marking the drama across Europe and America in the early 20th century. There is no single tendency—this is one of the most vibrant and varied periods of modern drama, as experimentation with all aspects of the drama abounds, including how plays are written (dramaturgy) as well as how they are staged (lighting, costume, scenery, acting).

Chekhov and Strindberg

In 1901, for example, two important yet strikingly different dramas appeared: Chekhov's *The Three Sisters* and Strindberg's *A Dream Play* (written in 1901, first performed 1907). Just as Ibsen's last play had departed considerably from his previous drama, *The Three Sisters* challenges all kinds of theatrical conventions. It resists melodrama, denies overt and causal action, and (perhaps due to Chekhov's training as a doctor) presents characters as objectively as possible.

Chekhov once wrote that on stage, 'everything should be as complex and as simple as in life'. While people are just eating their dinner, their future happiness is being decided or their lives are falling apart. *The Three Sisters* shows the gradual dispossession of a family from their home—it happens before our eyes, as each act shows the sisters moved one step further from their house, from the living room to the bedroom to the veranda to the garden. This sad trajectory happens amid uneventful, everyday conversation.

The combination of the climactic and the uneventful, the ordinary and the momentous, characterizes Chekhov's plays, but they are not mere exercises in nostalgia, even though characters often long for a past that seemed better and are paralysed in the present. 'What a difference between things as they are and as they were', sighs Vershinin, voicing a nostalgia that recurs in Samuel Beckett's plays in the 1950s such as *Endgame*, *Krapp's Last Tape*, and *Happy Days*. Yet Vershinin also looks forward, speculating about the future of the species, 'the life that will come after us in two or three hundred years'. Tuzenbach tartly responds: 'Life will remain just the same—difficult, full of mysteries, and happy. A thousand years from now man will still be sighing, "Ah, how hard life is!"—Yet he will fear death, exactly as he does now, and be unwilling to die.' This is the Chekhovian paradox, which accounts for the simultaneously tragic and comic quality of his work: the stasis that comes with the tug-of-war between the life force and the certainty of death in the knowledge that 'time is passing' and 'we shall be gone forever'.

Expressionism on stage

Strindberg's *A Dream Play* is radically different in its style of drama, an early example of expressionist theatre which flourished in the first few decades of the 20th century in Europe and later in America through plays like Eugene O'Neill's *The Emperor Jones* (1920), Elmer Rice's *The Adding Machine* (1923), and Sophie Treadwell's *Machinal* (1928).

Expressionist theatre is distorted and dreamlike, with exaggerated staging and characters that often seems mechanized or even fantastic, and there is often a heightened use of sound, lighting, and scenery to convey the central character's emotional state. For example, *Machinal* and *The Adding Machine* both use a soundscape reflecting the soul-destroying clatter of modern urban life—the persistent clacking of typewriters, the roar of the subway car—while in *The Emperor Jones* the rhythmic beating of drums conveys Jones's heartbeat, gradually accelerating as his desperate flight from his pursuers intensifies and suddenly stopping when he is shot.

In *A Dream Play*, a supernatural character—the daughter of the god Indra—journeys down from heaven to live among ordinary mortals and find out what it is like to be human. The play asks for non-realistic effects that can be hard to stage if taken too literally, such as a shawl that gathers human sorrows and cares throughout the play and a burning castle with a 'huge chrysanthemum' growing out of it and set against a wall of human faces. Scenes do not lead causally into each other. Instead of a continuous realistic setting, there are allegorical places such as Fairstrand (Heaven), Foulhaven (Hell), or a symbolic University, and in place of individualized characters with psychological depth there are archetypal figures simply called The Lawyer, The Poet, or The Glazier. Like the medieval morality play *Everyman*, the play didactically focuses the audience's attention on the ways in which each event or character in the play is a representative of a general human foible or sorrow.

Like the logic of a dream, Strindberg's play consists of seemingly unconnected episodes, all illustrating in different ways the central idea that humankind's tragedy is our desire *and* its fulfilment, and that:

> You miss what you never wanted;
> Regret even misdeeds never done.
> You want to leave, you want to stay;
> Your heart's drawn and quartered, torn apart
> By conflicting wishes, indecision, doubt.

Doubt is central to modernism, a movement that *A Dream Play* is part of: philosophical, religious, aesthetic, social, cultural doubt. Modern drama is one of the most powerful and eloquent genres for expressing and exploring this.

Intimate theatre and the Stanislavski revolution

Strindberg and Chekhov were both associated with the 'intimate theatre' or 'art theatre' movement represented by the many small, experimental theatres that sprang up during the late 19th and early 20th centuries including the Moscow Art Theatre, the Kammerspielhaus in Berlin, the Vieux-Colombier in Paris, the Intima Teatret in Stockholm, and the Provincetown Playhouse (inaugurated on the tip of Cape Cod, Massachusetts, then moving to Greenwich Village, New York). In 1916, this rickety little theatre poised on the edge of a wharf became the unlikely birthplace of modern American drama, establishing the Little Theatre Movement, influenced by the developments in Europe. It staged works by Glaspell, O'Neill, Edna St Vincent Millay, Djuna Barnes, Paul Green, Wallace Stevens, Theodore Dreiser, August Strindberg, and many others, and it is interesting to note that many were verse dramas, a form that the 'little theatre' movement briefly enabled.

Such theatres seemed the antithesis of the grand, new, neoclassical national theatres that had just opened across Europe, a key development of modern drama that links it directly to the expression of a collective, national identity. Instead, the 'intimate' or 'little' theatre movement focused on small spaces with tiny audiences in close proximity to the actors, breathing the same air, sharing the same room, which brought a new level of intensity and excitement to the theatrical experience. Integral to this movement was Constantin Stanislavski's development of a new theory of acting, which he put into practice in directing and acting in Chekhov's plays, among others, at the Moscow Art Theatre.

The Stanislavski method, which has had such a profound and lasting impact on modern acting across Europe and America (in both theatre and film), hinges on the actor's in-depth emotional development of his/her role. The actor must find emotional subtexts from his/her own experiences (the 'magic if') that can be deployed in inhabiting the role, and must flesh out the story of the character even when only sketchy details are given in the play, in order to develop a 'through-line of action'. Even if a character doesn't speak any lines in a certain scene, the actor still needs fully to inhabit the role and think about where in this line of action he/she sits.

One of the results of this new psychological approach was that even minor roles became important; even an 'extra' with no lines had a full backstory, a set of motives and desires, a reason for being in a particular scene. It wasn't just Chekhov's dramas that enabled this kind of acting. The Moscow Art Theatre's production of Maksim Gorky's *The Lower Depths* (1902)—notable for the novelty of showing the downtrodden underbelly of society (tramps in a run-down boarding house)—afforded great ensemble acting opportunities and a strikingly naturalistic set.

Another result of Stanislavski's system is a shift from plays featuring a central 'star' actor to those with a more balanced distribution of roles. *The Three Sisters* is not a star vehicle but an ensemble piece: most of the parts have equal weight. This is what Ibsen and Chekhov helped usher into modern European and

Russian drama, and it came to Britain in the form of Bernard Shaw and Harley Granville Barker's work at the Court Theatre in 1904–7.

Ensemble and repertory at the Court Theatre

Emphasizing repertory and ensemble acting over the old 'star system' of the actor-manager's theatre that prevailed in the 19th century, the Court put on new plays by Shaw, Granville Barker, and many other playwrights who otherwise might not have found a venue for their work. One of these was the American playwright, actress, and novelist Elizabeth Robins, whose suffrage play *Votes for Women!* (1907) illustrates one of the ways in which the Court helped to revolutionize the theatre in Britain—not only in the kinds of themes and characters it portrayed but in how theatre was *done*.

Superficially, the play doesn't seem all that innovative: it is essentially a well-made play that relies on the revelation of past sin and the motif of the 'fallen woman'. But this is all geared towards political action, and towards modelling how women can turn private experience into public good, rather than maintaining separate spheres. This is enacted in the central scene of the play, which takes place at a suffrage rally in Trafalgar Square before a hostile crowd of onlookers who heckle and jeer the speakers. These 'extras' all stand with their backs to the audience, so that they blend seamlessly with the audience rather than being separated from them by the proscenium arch. Even if some audience members might have been sympathetic to the suffrage cause, they had to experience what it was like to be among people who were not. The main speaker, Vida Levering, uses the tragic stories of 'women with a past'—including her own experiences—to persuade the crowd of the need for gender equality. 'It's not enough to be sorry for these unfortunate sisters. We must get the conditions of life made fairer. We women must organise. We must learn to work together.'

Chekhov's three sisters also speak of work as their saviour, the only thing worth doing in the end, yet either they don't do enough actual work or else get worn down by it. Vida closes *Votes for Women!* with the rousing invocation 'There is work to do', but with the difference that work is no longer abstract; the audience has experienced first hand its transformative effect on the people and events they are watching.

The Irish dramatic movement

At the same time, another theatrical movement of equal importance was taking root in Ireland, with the Irish National Theatre established in 1903 by W.B. Yeats, J.M. Synge, Lady Gregory, Annie Horniman, and others.

They had witnessed the impact of Ibsen on contemporary theatre and the chaotic effect of Jarry's *Ubu Roi*. They wanted to inject some of this foreign energy into Irish theatre, but to make it truly Irish by drawing on Celtic mythology and symbolism. In 1904 they opened the Abbey Theatre in Dublin. Yeats wrote many plays for the Abbey and helped shape it as its director. But, rather than Yeats's sometimes heavy-handed plays, it was the famous 'riots' over J.M. Synge's *Playboy of the Western World* (1907) that singled Ireland out as a leading site of new drama.

Synge's play built on vernacular speech (the Aran islands dialect) and his poetic ear to create a heightened, stylized English that sounded both familiar and strange when spoken by the ordinary Irish peasants of the play:

> CHRISTY: Amn't I after seeing the love-light of the star of knowledge shining from her brow, and hearing words would put you thinking on the holy Brigid speaking to the infant saints, and now she'll be turning again, and speaking hard words to me, like an old woman with a spavindy ass she'd have, urging on a hill. (Act II)

Though they speak lyrically, these peasants behave strangely: the main character, Christy Mahon, becomes a local hero in the town he's arrived at out of the blue when he boasts to the people that he has killed his father, his deed making him particularly attractive to the girls. When his father turns up alive and well—one of the great moments in modern drama—the local people are disgusted and disappointed with Christy, so he tries to finish off the deed properly in order to live up to his reputation as 'playboy of the western world'.

The play became a 'political battleground' when staged at the Abbey; Yeats received a telegram reporting that the 'audience broke up in disorder', because Synge's play allegedly besmirched Irish womanhood, depicted Irish peasants as gullible, and suggested that the Irish are morally skewed. The 'Playboy riots' have gone down in theatre history just as the first-night disturbances over Jarry's *Ubu Roi* had done a decade earlier.

Such riots suggest that theatre at this time really mattered. People cared about it in a way rarely seen since, writing passionately for or against particular plays in newspapers and showing their feelings at the theatre by making noise, 'shouting, stamping, and playing musical instruments' in some cases. But the term 'riots' isn't really accurate, because these disturbances were actually more like organized protests than disorderly disturbances. Audiences 'devised and enacted resistance through verbal rejoinders, physical gestures, and organized group demonstrations', writes theatre scholar Neil Blackadder; exactly what Robins captures in her play *Votes for Women!*.

Verse drama—a non-starter?

At the same time—showing how capacious and varied an art form modern drama is—there was a development that might be described as the polar opposite of such galvanizing, politically charged plays: the attempt to revive verse drama, which had languished for decades (remember Ibsen's renunciation of verse for the more modern cadences of prose). True, there could be poetry in even the grimmest of naturalistic plays; playwright and novelist John Galsworthy wrote of 'the poetry that lies in all vital things'. But others mourned what they saw as a loss of poetry in modern drama to what Synge called the 'joyless and pallid words' of Ibsen and Zola. As Synge saw it, 'in a good play every speech should be as fully flavoured as a nut or apple'.

Yeats, Synge, and many others sought to rectify this by resurrecting the poetic drama, or at least trying to inject more poetry into plays, largely through language but also through symbols that carried poetic weight, gesturing towards or invoking potent, universal ideas. Synge fused musicality and linguistic lushness with symbolism in his one-act play *Riders to the Sea* (1904), a tragic story of Maurya losing, one by one, her husband and five sons to the sea. The simple image of the relentless, unfeeling sea dominates the entire piece and even informs its structure, for in the midst of her keening and grief, Maurya sees old women entering her house to mourn with her for the lost men, and it is not clear whether they are real or imagined, whether her grief has taken her over the edge of sanity. The audience shares these visions with her and powerfully feels her sorrow.

The one-act play

Riders to the Sea has been called 'the greatest one-act tragedy in the English language'. It was part of a growing body of one-act dramas in this period that are remarkable for their effectiveness both on the stage and on the page. Eugene O'Neill, best known for his full-length plays (and often *very* long ones at that), started his career with one-act plays like *Bound East for Cardiff* (1914). J.M. Barrie, best known for the 1904 hit *Peter Pan*, worked repeatedly in the one-act form, in plays like *The Twelve Pound Look* (1914). Clearly there was audience appetite for a form that could compress so much into so little time and also fit nicely into an evening's varied entertainment, as one of several short plays or in combination with a longer piece. Often, their brevity also masked a political punch far above their weight.

Nowhere is this more evident than in one of the masterpieces of the genre: *Trifles* (1916) by the American playwright Susan Glaspell. *Trifles* is based on a true crime that Glaspell wrote about as a young reporter in Iowa. (Like Ibsen's use of Laura Kieler's story to create *A Doll's House*.) A farmer has been murdered in his house; the sheriff and his deputies are examining the premises for evidence while their wives wait in the kitchen. The men look all over the house but don't bother with the kitchen, because they assume it's 'just' a woman's space. The wives, however, and the audience watching them, gradually uncover the truth of what happened from trifling clues left in the kitchen—sloppily sewn quilting, neglected preserves, dirty dishcloths, general disorder—that enable them to piece together a tragic, though all too familiar, story of domestic abuse. 'Not much of a housekeeper, would you say, ladies?' remarks the County Attorney before leaving the 'mess' in the kitchen for more important areas of the house. Meanwhile, the 'ladies' have already realized that something is very wrong. The final, awful clue comes when they discover a dead canary hidden in a little box. They realize that Minnie Wright's husband killed it in an act of cruelty and that this was the last straw for her, driving the emotionally imprisoned woman to murder. 'Somebody—wrung—its—neck', says Mrs Peters, and *'Their eyes meet. A look of growing comprehension, of horror.'*

But this revelation doesn't just confirm Minnie's guilt. It also makes the women realize that they could have done more to help Minnie—they are, in some way, guilty of failing to reach out, hiding behind the excuse that 'she kept so much to herself'. Sisterhood is vital in a patriarchal world; 'I might have known she needed help', admits Mrs Hale, 'we live so close together and we live far apart. We all go through the same things.' The women's guilt and new-found solidarity is shown, not described, in such moments when they exchange meaningful looks that the men do not see but the audience does. The silent exchanges confirm their refusal to reveal what they know, even if, like Nora's forgery, that is a crime—they will stick with Minnie, a silent jury of her peers.

This thirty-minute play is often described as understated and restrained, because it uses only a few well-chosen props, lapses frequently into silences full of unspoken emotion, and avoids melodramatic touches. It is streamlined and spare in a way that later plays would take even further, giving silence, unfinished sentences, vagueness, and allusion a more central place in modern drama. *Trifles* subtly teaches the audience how to 'see' differently, from a woman's perspective. A gem of realism, it asks '*whose* realism?' It also asks what Ibsen's *A Doll's House* and Robins' *Votes for Women!* had asked too: 'how can a woman get a fair trial if she is not judged by a jury of her peers?' *Trifles* premiered the same year as *Rachel*, by Angelina Weld Grimké, about an African American woman's response to her father and brother's lynching; two female-authored plays representing the plight of women in America against a larger backdrop of social inequality. These plays were written at a time of intense agitation for women's suffrage and for rights for women more generally, and theatre was at the forefront of this movement, as *Trifles* subtly shows.

There were many other female playwrights besides Glaspell and Grimké writing at this time, yet so few get recognized. Theatre historian Katherine Kelly calls this 'the ghost effect', asking: 'How could the work of 4,700 women writing in the U.S. and England—to cite two national examples—be mislaid?' There are a number of possible reasons, including gender masking through pseudonym or misleading adoption of male names and, of course, prejudice, not just against women as writers but against the one-act play, a form often favoured by female playwrights though popular as well with male playwrights like Barrie, Synge, and O'Neill.

In fact, theatre played a key role in getting the vote for women, as the many 'suffrage dramas' of the period demonstrate—such as *Votes for Women!* and Cicely Hamilton and Christopher St John's

How the Vote Was Won, as well as plays not overtly about suffrage
that forced audiences to confront the dire inequality between men
and women, such as Gita Sowerby's *Rutherford and Son* and
Elizabeth Baker's *Chains*. Theatre could even, on occasion, directly
influence policy. *Justice* (1910) by John Galsworthy exerted such a
profound effect on the Home Secretary that he had the law on
solitary confinement of prisoners changed, after watching the
silent agony of a prisoner subjected to this treatment in the play.

Although such moments of stage realism were powerful, in
general realism had quickly gone from being a new and radical
aesthetic development to being seen as entrenched, conservative,
reactionary, and narrow. Realistic plays unquestioningly recycled
worn stereotypes: the simple-minded 'Uncle Tom' black character,
the drunken and garrulous Irishman, the mendacious Jew, the
disabled person (usually lame) with a heart of gold but no chance
of love or success. Dissatisfied with its inherently patriarchal,
white hegemonic manifestations, playwrights began exploring
alternatives, such as expressionism.

World War I

But the advent of World War I changed everything. Playwrights
and directors bemoaned the temporary halt to progress that this
cataclysmic event brought to the stage as to so many other areas of
life, as people understandably sought escape in the theatre, and
producers were happy to present the lighter side of life through
entertainment traditions like music hall, vaudeville, cabaret, and
variety shows which continued to thrive, especially in Britain,
during the war. These theatrical forms became important sources
for later playwrights such as Samuel Beckett, Joan Littlewood, and
John Osborne.

As the real figures showing millions, not thousands, of casualties
came in and the horror of new weapons of warfare such as air strikes
and mustard gas became clear, theatre was quick to reflect the mood

of despair. For instance, Gwen John shows the impact of war on a family in her one-act play *Luck of War* (1917). The heavily pregnant protagonist receives shocking news: her husband, whom she had assumed killed in the war, suddenly shows up one evening just as she is about to have dinner with her new partner, the father of her unborn child. Yet this does not interrupt the action; far from sitting down to have a chat about it (as in many a male-authored drama, including *A Doll's House*), she continues with her routine while they talk, getting dinner on the table while simultaneously having the discussion that will determine her own future and that of her children. This same sense of domestic routine and its centrality, for better or worse, in a woman's life is highlighted in *Trifles* to a chilling degree. The focus is not on the returning soldier (or, in *Trifles*, the dead farmer) but on the women, and they just don't have time to stop what they're doing in order to talk.

Yet for many, the devastation caused by war had the opposite effect. The loss of life was so staggeringly high and so senseless, the post-traumatic stress so profound—Europe in ruins, the depression in Germany so severe that a loaf of bread cost thousands of marks—how could one simply pick up the pieces and go on as normal? The movement of Dada arose in this climate of despair and anger. Dada was founded by Tristan Tzara in Zurich in 1916 and spread quickly across Europe (also flourishing in New York). It was closely tied to its cousin, surrealism. Both movements are non-realistic performance modes that have their basis in a fragmented, nonsensical structure. Dada is more like performance art: one event had Tzara sitting on a chair tearing up a newspaper while someone rang a bell; another involved the provocative reading of a 'Cannibal Manifesto' at which the outraged audience threw fruit at the stage. These gestures reflect the feeling of nihilism brought about by the war.

Shaw's *Heartbreak House* (1919), pointedly subtitled 'A Fantasia in the Russian manner', is a trenchant commentary on the aftermath of World War I. The play evokes Chekhov's bored upper-class characters who refuse to face a society that is changing and rendering them obsolete, as in *The Cherry Orchard* (1904). Shaw castigates the British for likewise wilfully ignoring, in their dreamy country houses, the ominous signs of war and thus change. The staging Shaw calls for is remarkable: a house in the form of a ship, owned by the ancient Captain Shotover, and serving as a metaphor for the ship of state drifting aimlessly on political waters. Characters in this 'ship' fall in and out of sleep, symbolizing their blinkered state. 'Can't you think of something that will murder half Europe at one bang?' Mrs Hushabye plaintively asks her ageing inventor father, because 'living at the rate we do, you cannot afford life-saving inventions'.

Shaw was, like Wilde, continuing and modernizing a long tradition of British comedy, with a particular use of witty epigrams pivoting on paradox, that can be traced back through Congreve, Fielding, and other Restoration theatre; Noel Coward would soon take it forward through a new generation. In addition to *Heartbreak House*, Shaw's key plays during these decades include *Man and Superman* (1903), *John Bull's Other Island* (1904), *Major Barbara* (1905), *The Doctor's Dilemma* (1906), and *Pygmalion* (1912), and he had already published many plays in the 1890s as well as theatre criticism. The hallmark of his theatre work is its nimble and witty language as well as its often daring innovation in dramatic structure, length of plays, and in using the stage space.

Sex, censorship, and the avant-garde

Shaw was deeply committed to battling theatre censorship, and along with other leading theatre critics, directors, and playwrights he lobbied constantly for its abolition. But the iron hand of theatrical censorship prevailed, and it makes these decades as much a record of what *wasn't* seen on stage as what *was*. Edward Garnett's *The Breaking Point*, Harley Granville Barker's *Waste*, Marie Stopes's *Vectia*, and many other plays were refused licences because they all dealt frankly with a controversial sexual issue—such as abortion, sexual intercourse, or family planning—and were therefore deemed too unsavoury for stage representation. Britain was not alone: many other countries, including Russia, France, and Germany, also still had forms of theatre censorship, exercised to different degrees.

Already in 1903 Guillaume Apollinaire had written a play called *Les Mamelles de Tirésias* (*The Breasts of Tiresias*) that dealt openly with these same sexual issues, though it wasn't performed until 1917. One of the earliest surrealist dramas, the play features 'a man who makes children', 40,049 of them in fact, while his equally gender-bending wife grows a beard and loses her breasts (staged using balloons). The grotesque, exaggerated breasts don't seem linked to anything either sexual or nurturing. *Les Mamelles de Tirésias* belongs both to the kind of drama written by Jarry (discussed in Chapter 1) and to the much later movement of absurdism (Chapter 5).

Also avant-garde in style was *The Fairground Booth*, a collaboration between poet and playwright Aleksandr Blok and director Vsevolod Meyerhold in 1906. Meyerhold is a towering figure in modern drama. His innovations as a director spanned several decades, from roughly 1900 until 1940, when he was executed on Stalin's orders. *The Fairground Booth* fused ancient, cross-cultural theatrical traditions—puppet figures (the French Pierrot, Columbine, and Harlequin, and the Russian Petrushka), *grand guignol* (Punch and Judy shows), and *commedia dell'arte* (a Renaissance dramatic style using stock characters and improvisational techniques)—in modern form, and set a key precedent for several developments I discuss in this book: Pirandello's dramas, Meyerhold's stylized 'biomechanics', and Gordon Craig's 'übermarionette'. Like *Les Mamelles de Tirésias*, *The Fairground Booth* defiantly rejects the growing entrenchment of realism by embracing such devices to challenge the naturalism and corporeality of the actor's body, suggesting instead a puppet-like, non-human quality, and using archetype rather than individualized, psychologically deep characterization.

39

In 1907, Meyerhold directed the Russian premiere of the German playwright Frank Wedekind's *Spring Awakening*, written in 1891 but banned for fifteen years in Germany due to its frank treatment of adolescent sexuality, including masturbation, homosexuality, sadomasochism, rape, and allusions to abortion. The play is notable not only for its bold subject matter but for Wedekind's use of cabaret techniques such as ballad singing and an episodic structure; these would influence the young Bertolt Brecht. Meyerhold's direction emphasized these qualities and avoided social realism—he wrote in a production note that he wanted to 'tone down' the physical aspects of puberty depicted in the play, going instead for a 'soft, unemphatic tone' and contrasting the 'sunlight and joyousness' of the setting with the 'chaos and gloom' of the adolescents. The innovation of this production appealed to theatre makers everywhere; the Stage Society produced the play a few years later in London (1910).

Yet London was no longer the sole home of theatrical dominance in Britain. At the Gaiety Theatre in Manchester, founded and funded by Annie Horniman after her successful venture with the Abbey Theatre in Dublin, the 'Manchester school' of playwrights flourished: these included Harold Brighouse, Stanley Houghton, and Allan Monkhouse. Their plays helped to initiate a strong regionalism that continued to grow throughout subsequent decades and still thrives today.

Stage craft

Not just the themes but the aesthetics of the stage also radically changed. Adolphe Appia experimented with lighting, manipulating colour and shade to create 'living' sets that abolished the visual trickery of painted scenery in favour of non-naturalistic, symbolic, and abstract staging. Edward Gordon Craig envisioned a theatre liberated from its enslavement to physicality, with marionettes rather than actors. Strindberg, Wedekind, and others brought expressionism to the stage and Stanislavski's acting system continued to take hold, eventually sweeping across the Western theatre. Yet at the same time, Yeats drew inspiration from non-Western traditions like Noh theatre and the Dadaist movement integrated African masks into its theatrical vision.

This is the period when we begin to see theories of drama coming to the fore, often in tandem with plays that exemplify them and put them into practice. One of the results of modernist theatre's 'creative destructions', in Ackerman and Puchner's words, is that 'manifestoes, theatres and theories can no longer be neatly kept apart'. Craig's *On the Art of the Theatre* (1911) ushered in a new way of thinking about the stage and the actor. He challenged the dominance of realism by suggesting replacing real actors with puppets and by embracing the use of masks, among other devices. There is a direct link between his ideas and those of Meyerhold, Artaud, Brecht, and Piscator: all have in common a dissatisfaction with realistic acting, and with the unquestioning way that realistic plays relate to their audiences. These important practitioners would each seek to renovate and remake drama through their own challenges to the conventions of the stage.

These plays and performances show the extraordinary interweaving of the two main strands of political agitation and aesthetic innovation that characterized the theatre of these decades. So many of the key moments in modern drama in these years happened briefly and were short-lived; it is one of the distinctive features of the genre, much like the fleeting lives of many modernist 'little magazines'. It is totally in keeping with the experimental nature of modern art generally, and of modernism.

In short, during the decades 1900–20 theatre arguably enjoyed its greatest cultural relevance and centrality—even as the new art form of cinema (itself deeply influenced by theatre) was taking hold and radically challenging that status.

Chapter 3
Metatheatre and modernity

The period 1920–40 is the flowering of high modernism, which
involved radical innovation and experimentation across literature
and the arts including the theatre. Many felt that realism had
become boring and predictable, a state of affairs reinforced by the
rise of film which also became relentlessly mimetic despite its
initial exuberant and creative promise and the many notable
experiments with cinematic form. (Such experiments were often
inspired by theatre or indeed inspired the theatre, but there is
regrettably no space here to tell that story.)

In the theatre, dramatists and directors challenged the growing
entrenchment of realism, rebelling against an illusion of
reality that hypnotizes the audience and makes it passive.
Instead, they wanted to unsettle the comfortable assumptions
of the audience, but each for very different reasons, some
ideological and political, some primarily aesthetic. Dramatists
in these decades stretched audiences' expectations and
imaginations as never before, and introduced ever more daring
subject matter and characterization. One of the most important of
these is Bertolt Brecht, to whom a large part of the discussion
here is devoted, as he is such a towering figure in modern
drama. But others are important too, beginning with Luigi
Pirandello.

Reinventing metatheatre

Italian playwright Luigi Pirandello came to the theatre belatedly, after a successful career as a novelist and short-story writer, but his late entrance was sensational. His play *Six Characters in Search of an Author* (written in the late teens) was staged in Rome in 1921, London and America in 1922, Paris in 1923, and Berlin in 1924—each production under a different iconoclastic director, each notable in its own way. The premiere at the Teato Valle in Rome had a tumultuous reception, with the audience divided into supporters and opponents, echoing the premiere of Jarry's *Ubu Roi* and the *Playboy* riots discussed in Chapters 2 and 3. In response, Pirandello extensively reworked the play in subsequent versions.

The play used the age-old form of metatheatre, radically reimagined for the modern stage as an antidote to realism. Into the middle of a rehearsal for a Pirandello play (a strange metatheatrical reference for the audience) wander six characters from an unfinished drama abandoned by its author. They have a compelling story to tell and they ask the actors and director to set aside the play they have been rehearsing in order to act out the characters' drama and thereby find closure and completion to what reveals itself to be a very traumatic story. The actors end up staging the characters' drama—a play within a play—which unsettles the audience, blurring the line between spectator and actor, questioning what is illusion and what is reality. Along the way, the dialogue constantly exposes the weaknesses in conventional theatre and, by analogy, in real life, as full communication of our inner selves is utterly impossible. Shaking with anger, the Producer, who is trying to stage the characters' drama, rages at their impossible demands:

> I know perfectly well that we've all got a life inside us and that we
> all want to parade it in front of other people. But that's the difficulty,
> how to present only the bits that are necessary in relation to the

other characters: and in the small amount we show, to hint at all the rest of the inner life! (Act II)

It would be so much simpler, he says, if each character could simply give a soliloquy pouring out to the audience 'what's bubbling away inside him'. But 'that's not the way we work'. An old model of theatre must give way to a new one founded on restraint.

Pirandello wanted the two groups (actors and characters) to look utterly distinct from one another, and asked in his stage directions that the characters wear masks ('made so that the eyes, the nose and the mouth are all free'). This interest in masks was shared by other modern dramatists like Eugene O'Neill, and is part of the strain of modern theatre that centres around the non-naturalistic, even non-human form, from Gordon Craig's übermarionette through to the stylized techniques of the Asian theatre that inspired Yeats, Brecht, and Artaud.

In 'Alienation Effects in Chinese Acting' (1936), Brecht described how the acting is done in such a way that the audience consciously accepts or rejects the actions and speech of the characters, instead of subconsciously. Brecht was deeply influenced by seeing the techniques of Mei Lanfang, one of the most influential Beijing (then Peking) opera artists of modern times. Artaud loved Balinese theatre (Figure 2) for similar reasons (though he sometimes misunderstood the motivations behind it) and Yeats and O'Neill were both influenced by Japanese Noh theatre (Figure 3). The stylized, codified nature of gestures, the use of metonymy—all challenged realism and all held out a possibility of recapturing what Artaud termed theatre's 'magic'.

The simple structure of *Six Characters*—having a director on stage instructing a set of characters what to do—has also been used by subsequent dramatists, including Brecht in *The Caucasian Chalk Circle* (1944) and Brian Friel in *Living Quarters* (the 'director' figure in this play even holds the master script—the 'book'—with

2. A Balinese *legong* dancer holds elbows high, changes position dynamically and uses piercing, darting eye expression, giving an energized image of the female.

which he directs the others); and in *Copenhagen* (1998) Michael Frayn's self-directing characters agree to re-enact a fateful meeting in order to arrive at the difficult and elusive truth about it. Life is a kind of role-playing and there is no director so we have to invent one.

Pirandello's plays are a powerful exploration of the line between sanity and insanity, reality and illusion, and they collectively comment on the theatricality of life as we inhabit roles that obscure our true selves.

The other great modern reinventor of metatheatre, the German playwright Bertolt Brecht, built up a long career spanning over three decades, from around 1920 until his death in 1956, and left an even longer legacy. Both playwrights chafe against the comfortable illusions of realism and want to provoke their audiences, but where Pirandello's aesthetic is philosophically inclined (exploring

3. Japanese Noh theatre fuses voice, narrative, action, dance, and
music, but keeps each strand of the performance separate, giving the
spectator the sense of these elements constantly shifting in relation to
one another.

the idea of the fundamental theatricality of life), Brecht's is
informed by ideology, politics, and the desire to change society.
And where Pirandello lavishes words (both in the dialogue and
the stage directions)—indeed, making words into 'spoken
action' as he called it—Brecht uses language more sparingly,
leavening it with a range of other elements like music and
screen projections. Though both are metatheatrical—calling
attention to the theatre as theatre—they are very different in their
uses of this concept.

Observation, analysis, and change

Brecht's work falls into three phases: the first phase is 'epic',
lasting until the end of the 1920s; the second is *Verfremdung*
(roughly 1930s–1940s); and the third is the retrospective

codification of his ideas and practices. Since the codification came after the playwriting, it is important to approach Brecht first through his plays and then through his theories, beginning with his attempts at distancing the audience.

Lots of people know the catchy tune 'Mack the Knife' made famous by Louis Armstrong, Frank Sinatra, and other crooners. But they may not realize that this song, itself a translation by Marc Blitzstein, originally came from a collaboration by Brecht and Kurt Weill, *The Threepenny Opera* (1928, Figure 4). Influenced by fellow German Erwin Piscator, Brecht's early theatre is steeped in popular forms of drama and music, such as ballads, street theatre, and music hall. Like the German composer Richard Wagner (1813–1883, discussed in Chapter 1), Brecht was interested in how music, and specifically opera, could be used in the theatre, but for deeply divergent purposes—whereas Wagner aspired to a

4. The scaffold scene of Bertolt Brecht's *The Threepenny Opera* in its original 1928 staging with epic elements such as bare stage and placard announcing the scene title and substance.

complete synthesis of the elements of theatre (text, music, staging), Brecht aimed for a separation of all of these elements. Music is used to interrupt the action and comment sharply on it, rather than serving as an atmospheric accompaniment that lulls the audience.

The Threepenny Opera is a modern reworking of John Gay's *The Beggar's Opera* (1728), and is, like Gay's original, an anti-opera. It depicts the underclass of London led by villain and anti-hero Macheath, who marries Polly Peachum against her father's wishes; in revenge, her father has him captured and sentenced to be hanged. At the last minute, he is given a reprieve, and the carnivalesque atmosphere of the celebrations highlights the extent to which this is a parody of the (usually implausible) happy endings of so much theatre and opera. Brecht and Weill intersperse ballads and songs that interrupt the action as well as comment on it and draw attention in an entertaining way to some endemic problems in society, such as class inequality. The audience enjoys the music but doesn't get too caught up in the action because it is constantly being interrupted in the process of identifying with the main character, Polly, and her plight.

Like *The Threepenny Opera*, many of Brecht's works were collaborations; all his creative life Brecht worked with others, believing strongly in collaborative working practice, and in this way he also influenced subsequent dramatists—for example, Joan Littlewood and Ewan MacColl in Theatre Workshop (1950s–1960s) and Caryl Churchill's workshopping process with the Joint Stock Theatre Company later on. This process ensures that multiple perspectives feed into the play—a dialectical process at the heart of Brecht's theatrical vision.

Distancing the audience

The songs, gestures, placards, lack of scenery, and interrupted actions that Brecht experimented with in works like *The Threepenny Opera* were all part of his aim to prevent the audience from getting too absorbed in the action and emotions of the characters. This distancing would retain the audience's capacity to think about and analyse what it was seeing on stage, and perhaps leave the theatre with a clearer idea of what the problems in society were and how they could be solved.

Brecht began using the term *Verfremdungseffekt* in the mid-1930s. It is his own original term, strongly influenced by Karl Marx's term *Entfremdung*, which described the alienation of the worker from the means of production. Brecht, however, does not seek total alienation of audience from work. 'A representation producing *Verfremdung*,' he writes, 'is one that allows us to recognize an object, but at the same time makes it appear strange.' This idea had already gained critical currency with the Russian formalist Viktor Shklovsky's concept of defamiliarization or estrangement (articulated in his 'Art as Technique' essay in 1925). Brecht realized that one way of achieving this kind of distance and forestalling too much emotion is to have a narrator; for example, *Man is Man* (1924) has a prologue that asserts an authorial voice right from the start of the play, and many of his other plays have similar kinds of commentary, or running narrative, on the action.

Verfremdung is the beginning of a cognitive process that continues long after the audience has left the theatre. Having witnessed the deconstruction of its habitual performance codes and the hostility to dominant institutions, societal forces, and cultural norms, the audience of a Brecht play should sense the possibility of change because it has seen that, as theatre scholar Janelle Reinelt puts it, 'history is not an inevitable narrative'. If we can change the status quo, we can change the direction of the narrative of history as we are living it. Human beings 'do not have to stay the way they are; they may be looked at not only as they are now, but also as they might be'.

Two further examples of Brecht's work illustrate this. *Mother Courage and Her Children* (1938–9; produced 1941) and *Life of*

Galileo (written in 1937–9; revised in 1940s and again in 1955 for the last time) are among Brecht's most famous works for the stage, and are among the most regularly revived plays in his repertoire. Both plays depict devastating events. In *Mother Courage*, a mother's three grown children die one by one in circumstances she either helped unwittingly to bring about or that she could have prevented. *Galileo* shows the decline into blindness, obscurity, and old age of the once-vital scientist who seems to have 'sold out' both his country and his science. Both plays have strong central characters going through profoundly wrenching experiences; it is the stuff of tragedy, like *Hamlet* or *Oedipus Rex*, and in a conventional dramatist's hands it would move us to tears.

But Brecht forestalls too much identification with the characters. Instead of getting swept away in cathartic emotion, we think about the forces that brought the events about in the first place—things *external* to character. Using an episodic structure, ballads, and historical materials (both *Mother Courage* and *Galileo* are set in the early 17th century and loosely reimagine real events), he keeps us at just enough of a remove from the action to engage our brains but not too much emotion. In *Galileo*, for instance, he does not dramatize the famous moment in court when Galileo buckled under the threat of torture and said that the sun moves around the earth, but then whispered to himself the famous words 'And yet, it [the earth] moves'. Instead, he keeps the courtroom doors firmly shut and shows only a small group of Galileo's friends and students waiting outside, expecting Galileo to be heroic and defy the authorities in order to uphold his heliocentric theory. When they learn that he has given in, some of them are disgusted and feel he has betrayed science as well as his country. 'Unhappy is the land that breeds no hero', says his former student, to which Galileo retorts: 'Unhappy is the land that needs a hero'. Brecht's Galileo also seems to be the slave of his physical needs for food, wine, and comfort ('I don't think well unless I eat well ... I get my best ideas over a good meal and bottle of wine'). But this is meant to show not that Galileo is a weak glutton, but that human beings—and their ideas—are tied to material conditions.

Brecht isn't against the audience experiencing emotion; identification with the characters is important to him, just not to the extent that it obscures rational thought. When Mother Courage loses her third child, Katrin, who is shot while bravely beating a drum on the roof of a hut in an attempt to warn her community of the arrival of enemy soldiers, she says 'God, I hate the war'. She *says* it; she doesn't cry it out with anguish; it is a statement of fact, not a melodramatic or tragic moment. This reflects Brecht's aim of a dialectical theatre in which the audience watches opposing viewpoints clashing and has to judge for itself which is right. As he put it in his manifesto 'Short Organon for the Theatre' (1948, though it went through three versions), 'imagine a man standing in a valley and making a speech in which he occasionally changes his opinion or simply utters sentences that contradict one another, so that the accompanying echo brings them into confrontation'.

Elsewhere, he likens the audience of 'epic' plays to spectators at a boxing match: one of the opponents is going to win, but both deserve to if they are equally good. The spectators are able to watch with a certain detachment, not thinking too empathetically about the combatants. Brecht uses such analogies as theatrical thought-experiments to train his audiences to think differently, just as scientists use such techniques to solve problems.

Similarly, gesture for Brecht is the reflection of external relations, not the expression of internal emotional states. Plays are, quite simply, 'our representations of the way people live together'. The human condition has changed radically from what it was a few hundred years ago, before the Industrial Revolution and the current 'scientific age', so theatre must begin to reflect this fundamental change. In place of the old-fashioned 'dramatic' theatre of suspense and catharsis, then, Brecht proposed an 'epic theatre' (see Table 1).

Table 1

Dramatic form of theatre	Epic form of theatre
Action	Narration
Involves spectators in events on stage	Turns spectators into observers
Consumes their activity	Awakens their activity
Enables them to have feelings	Forces them to make decisions
Experience	World-picture
The spectators are immersed in something	The spectators are put in opposition to something
Suggestibility	Argument
Emotions are preserved	Emotions are turned into insights
The spectator stands right in the middle	The spectator stands on the opposite side
The spectator shares in the experience	The spectator studies
Human nature presumed to be common knowledge	Human nature is object of investigation
Humankind unchangeable	Humankind changeable and able to change things
Tension at the outcome	Tension as you go
One scene for the next	Each scene for itself
Growth	Montage
Structure of events linear	Structure of events in curves
Evolutionary inevitability	Jumps
Human nature as fixed	Human nature as process
Thought determines being	Social being determines thought
Feeling	Rationality

How should an actor do all of this? In my discussion of Brechtian theatre so far, a lot of the emphasis has been on changing the way plays are written and the way audiences respond to them. But the real burden of change lies on the actor. For all of these aims to be achieved, the actor has to throw away the Stanislavski method by which he transforms himself totally into the character. Brecht worked hard with the actors in his company, the Berliner Ensemble, to combat what he felt was the 'excessive' empathy dominating contemporary acting. An actor should not disappear into the role but maintain a distance from it: 'All he has to do is show his character'. In doing so, he does not obliterate himself; and by not identifying with the character's feelings he makes the audience always aware that he is acting, and that there are many other possible interpretations of the character on display, and many other possible outcomes of the events depicted. Most important is to show how acting, and by extension living life, involves a process, not a finished product. This is what Brecht did when working with the American actor Charles Laughton in his role as Galileo in 1947, one of the best examples of Brechtian acting on record.

Brecht's career is so significant that full discussion of it will continue in Chapter 4, which deals with the period when he and his collaborators produced some of his most important work for the stage and most influential theories about theatre. Many of these techniques had already been introduced into German theatre by Erwin Piscator, culminating in his book *The Political Theatre* (1929) which was important for elucidating the concept of 'epic' theatre. Piscator's other techniques included using still and cinematic projections and complex scaffolding in place of a box set.

Throughout the 1940s, Piscator lived in America and taught an influential theatre workshop (some of his students would become some of Hollywood's finest actors: Bea Arthur, Marlon Brando, Tony Curtis, Rod Steiger, Elaine Stritch). Another student he taught in this Dramatic Workshop was Tennessee Williams. Piscator profoundly shaped modern drama, especially in America. Together, Pirandello, Piscator, and Brecht show how well theatre lends itself to artistically exploring the vexed issue of what reality is and what illusion is, since traditionally theatre relies on hiding the fact that it is delivering 'mere' illusion.

Women's voices

There is a natural affinity between feminism and epic theatre. Both question assumptions behind realism, asking '*whose* realism?' Both want to disrupt easy identification, getting audiences to think and analyse and then to change the status quo. The period 1920–40 witnessed a surge of new plays by women, and many, understandably, dealt with feminist concerns. Glaspell's *The Verge* (1921), her best-known full-length play, is remarkable not just for its use of expressionist techniques and its unusual staging (the first part of the play takes place in a greenhouse full of strange, hybrid plants that a female botanist is cultivating), but also for pioneering a female language, a kind of theatrical *l'écriture féminine* ('woman's writing'). Claire Archer, the botanist trying to create new plant forms, also creates a new way of expressing herself, as her disjointed, fragmented speeches show her struggling to break out of a dead patriarchal language that is inadequate. Her language becomes a kind of resistance to language itself:

> Break this up—it can't go farther. In the air above—in the sea
> below—it is to kill! All we had thought we were—we aren't. We
> were shut in with what wasn't so. Is there one ounce of energy has
> not gone to this killing? Is there one love not torn into two?
> Throw it in! Now? Ready? Break up. Push. Harder. Break up. And
> then—and then— (Act I)

Claire's husband tells her: 'you have the most preposterous way of using words'. She likens words to plants. She moves abruptly from prose to verse. She uses oddly ungrammatical constructions, speaking as if she doesn't know how to speak, and she says 'um, um' at climactic moments. She resents words that 'smother' and she makes up words, like 'fartherness'. Glaspell goes further than any previous playwright in attempting to *stage* women's states of mind and emotion: to use silence that speaks, to use inarticulateness heavy with implicit meaning. The play's tragic ending shows the toll that living inside an alien language and culture takes: Claire rejects everyone around her, including her own grown-up, comfortably conservative daughter, declaring that she wishes she had never had her; and she kills her lover Tom, the only person who seems to understand her.

The Verge was well received in England when it premiered there in 1924: critics called it 'groundbreaking', 'a brilliant psychological study', 'a great play, to be considered alongside those of Ibsen', and hailed Glaspell as 'the greatest playwright writing in English since Shaw began'. Like her fellow Modernist Djuna Barnes, especially Barnes' highly experimental play *The Dove* (1923), Glaspell's theatrical work shows the influence of Ibsen, Synge, and, in turn, French symbolist theatre, particularly Maeterlinck in her use of the symbolically named 'Edge Vine' and 'Breath of Life' and in her attempt to indicate inner struggle, to show silent 'soul states' dramatically. But she is constantly, restlessly trying to move beyond these influences, to develop something new out of them.

Another playwright who powerfully depicts the plight of women is the Spanish writer Federico García Lorca, best known internationally for his 'rural trilogy': *Blood Wedding* (1932), *Yerma* (1934), and *The House of Bernarda Alba* (1936; first production 1945). These plays challenged social norms of bourgeois Spanish society such as narrowly proscribed roles for women, homophobia, and a rigid class structure. They dramatize the cost of repressing natural human urges in an effort to conform to outmoded codes of behaviour. Though much of Lorca's earlier work explores other themes and experiments with many different theatrical styles (among them surrealism—see Box 2—as in *The Public*, 1930;

When Five Years Pass, 1931; *Play Without a Title*, 1935), in these last three plays of his career he turns to the predicament of women as a powerful and urgent theme of modern drama.

'To be born a woman's the worst possible punishment', says Amelia in *The House of Bernarda Alba* (Figure 5), a play that has no men in it at all. Bernarda Alba is a tyrant: grieving for her dead husband, she imposes eight years of mourning on her household of women consisting of her five grown daughters, her mother, and their maids. She forces them to wear black incessantly, she obsessively keeps the house scoured white, she even gags her elderly mother so that she will not shout. Thumping a big stick constantly as she walks, she makes life a prison for them all and eventually drives her youngest daughter, Adela, to suicide.

Box 2 Surrealism

Surrealism was another important theatrical trend during the 1920s–1940s, and it grew out of Dada performance art in the teens. Guillaume Apollinaire coined the term when he dubbed his play *The Breasts of Tiresias* (1917) a 'surrealist' drama. 'Sur' means 'on top of' or 'above', not 'under' as is sometimes mistakenly assumed. This suggests not only a subterranean, unconscious world but also a world *above* reality, as in dreams; one that can be sunlit, light-hearted, and whimsical as well as psychologically dark.

The Breasts of Tiresias revels in the humorous, the grotesque and the incongruous, primarily by collapsing gender distinctions (a husband has thousands of babies; a mad doctor prescribes universal abortion) and by innovative staging (a woman's breasts fly off her body as balloons).

Other key theatrical surrealists are Lorca, Antonin Artaud, Jacques Cocteau, and Gertrude Stein, for example in her opera *Doctor Faustus Lights the Lights* (1938).

5. Domestic oppression: the menacing and destructive interplay between the generations of women in Lorca's *The House of Bernarda Alba*, in a 2007 production at the Centro Cultural de la Villa Madrid, Spain.

Even this new anguish cannot dim her desire to repress them all. 'And I want no weeping. Death must be looked at face to face. Silence! Be still, I said! Silence, silence!'

Just as in Glaspell's *The Verge*, the hatred between women is both palpable and surprising. How can these plays be feminist if they show women turning on each other? What happened to the plea for sisterhood that was so strong in suffrage plays like *Votes for Women!*? Lorca shows the cost of living in a patriarchal and implicitly fascist society. It is precisely because Bernarda unquestioningly replicates male values and procedures that her world collapses; women don't fit it. These plays show the need for outlets for female talent and potential; the need, as Ibsen had suggested in *A Doll's House*, for women to create their own identities rather than simply put on the 'masquerade dress' men clothe them in; and to be judged by a 'jury of their peers'.

Political theatre

Clearly, one of the outstanding developments in these decades was the emergence of various kinds of *political* theatre, whether Brechtian, feminist, or socialist. This is a particularly strong tendency in British and Irish theatre, led by the Irish playwright Sean O'Casey. His Dublin Trilogy, consisting of *The Shadow of a Gunman* (1923), *Juno and the Paycock* (1924), and *The Plough and the Stars* (1926), shows a surface naturalism as each play depicts working-class life and is politically engaged, but in addition, and much like Shaw, O'Casey is interested in experimenting with theatrical styles and challenging audience expectations. This is especially clear in *The Silver Tassie* (1929) which, after a naturalistic opening act, switches abruptly into expressionist mode, as symbolism and realism co-exist.

O'Casey was also important in what has been called 'regional' theatre, encompassing Irish (O'Casey) and Scottish (Joe Corrie) playwrights, and the Manchester school mentioned in Chapter 2, as well as the establishment of permanent theatres, many of which are still going strong today (Abbey Theatre, Gaiety Theatre, Royal Court). From 1925 onwards the Abbey Theatre in Ireland received financial support from the Irish Free State, making it the first government-subsidized theatre in the English-speaking world. Others would follow suit: in the mid-1930s, Hallie Flanagan Davis became the first director of the Federal Theatre Project (FTP, 1935–9, during the years of the Depression when millions of people were out of work).

America's first and only successful attempt at a national theatre, the FTP reached millions of spectators across the United States through its productions, giving new meaning to the term 'regionalism': at its peak it employed 10,000 people and had theatres in forty states. The FTP developed its own original topical dramas, called 'living newspapers', modelled on Russian examples that Davis had seen first-hand. Part documentary and part fiction, they drew on actual sources—books, newspaper articles, courtroom proceedings—to create compelling drama addressing pressing issues of the day.

Three popular Living Newspaper plays were *Triple-A Plowed Under*, on the need for farmers and consumers to unite for improved incomes and cheaper food; *Power*, a plea for public ownership of utilities; and *One-Third of a Nation*, an exposé of urban housing conditions. The FTP's productions also addressed racism, health care, labour unions, and the use of natural resources. These may sound like dull, undramatic subjects, but the FTP made them fresh, innovative, and galvanizing. Each Living Newspaper script also carried the instruction that it should be changed and adapted to bring it up to date each time it was revived, keeping the essential core but ensuring its freshness and renewed relevance to new audiences.

With such openly progressive material and such vast audiences, the FTP inevitably fell victim to the growing 'red scare' in America, a right-wing campaign to eradicate communism that especially targeted playwrights, directors, and actors (the House Un-American Activities Committee, or HUAC, interrogated Arthur Miller, Bertolt Brecht, Elia Kazan, and many other leading theatre and film figures)—a deeply disturbing moment of American history that Miller dramatized in 1953 in his play *The Crucible*. It is ironic that the FTP, whose purpose was to produce 'free, adult, uncensored theatre', was closed down under the same administration that had set it up, as some members of Congress had become suspicious of the openly progressive orientation of its plays.

But Davis's work with the FTP has had a long and productive legacy. Not only did she leave behind a vision of theatre as a vibrant social institution that must dare to be dangerous, she showed that theatrical experimentation could be done on a large scale. And she helped launch the careers of, among others, director Orson Welles, actor Joseph Cotton, playwrights Paul Green and Arthur Miller, and composer Virgil Thompson. Theatre critic Harold Clurman later looked back at the FTP as 'the most truly experimental effort ever undertaken in the American theatre' and at the theatre of the 1930s as a model that

> reflected what was going on in the world around it...often verbose, hotheaded, loudmouthed, bumptious and possibly 'pretentious', [it] did not produce communism in our midst; it produced a creative ferment that is still the best part of whatever we have in our present strangulated and impractical theatre. We should look back to the groups, projects, collectives and 'unions' of the theatrical thirties, not simply with nostalgia, but with thoughts of emulation and renewal.

Indeed, the Living Newspaper model lived on through theatre directors like the Brazilian Augusto Boal, who reinvented it for his groundbreaking Theatre of the Oppressed in which audiences helped to decide the subject matter of the play, allowing for a more participatory kind of theatre that made the audience what Boal called 'spect-actors'.

Family secrets

All of this vitality and innovation left its mark on some playwrights, like Thornton Wilder, who wanted to import epic techniques into American drama. Though Wilder's *Our Town* (1938) and *The Skin of Our Teeth* (1941) are distinctly different in their subject matter, they both use epic techniques to disrupt easy identification and to pose sharp questions directly to the audience. *The Skin of Our Teeth* takes an epic look at human evolution, combining humour and tragedy with Brechtian techniques. *Our Town* uses a Stage Manager who narrates and directs the play, an affable presence who nonetheless keeps a cool and critical eye on the scenes of New Hampshire life he is showing us.

Largely because of its saccharine treatment in the Hollywood film version, complete with white picket fence and sentimental musical score, *Our Town* has often been misunderstood as a celebration of rural life and solid American values. But this seemingly simple story of two families brought together by the marriage of their children is actually a searing critique of narrowness, provinciality, and an attitude to childrearing that totally lacks empathy and understanding of child psychology—very similar to what Arthur Miller would do in *Death of a Salesman* a decade later. Wilder sets the play's moving final act in the afterlife, allowing the deceased Emily to relive certain moments from her past just as Jimmy Stewart does in the popular film *It's a Wonderful Life* (1946), to see not just what a difference she made in other people's lives but what opportunities she missed.

Wilder may have helped introduce a strong tradition in American drama of focusing on the family and its dark, destructive secrets, but he was doing so in a critical manner, using epic techniques to distance the audience and cause greater awareness of the societal forces shaping the family's behaviour. Eugene O'Neill, the other main instigator of the focus on the family, was far more interested in probing—often relentlessly—the psychology of the individual family members.

O'Neill is, perhaps unfairly, given the bulk of the blame for generating what Benedict Nightingale has disparagingly called the American 'diaper drama', plays that focus too narrowly on domestic life, family secrets, and dysfunctional parent–child relationships, and don't seem to bother with wider political issues. Many of O'Neill's plays do take us on long journeys through emotionally draining terrain, unearthing deep, destructive family secrets, just as Ibsen did in plays like *A Doll's House*, *The Wild Duck*, and *Ghosts*. In *Long Day's Journey into Night* and *A Moon for the Misbegotten* (both written in 1941), for instance, O'Neill shows the negative forces at work in families that suppress children's yearnings and needs, and provides deep psychological development of characters in essentially naturalistic mode. Nightingale asks: why should we care about these spoilt little characters and their petty problems?

But O'Neill's earlier phase showed how varied and politically engaged he could be, and how innovative with dramatic forms. We have seen how *The Emperor Jones* (1920) helped explode old, stereotypical roles for African American actors and utilized innovative expressionist techniques. *The Hairy Ape* (1922) likewise combines naturalistic and expressionistic devices and has an episodic structure. With *Desire Under the Elms* (1924), O'Neill dared to depict incest and infanticide on stage, and he set the play in a New England environment that demanded constant use of heavy dialect. His play *Strange Interlude* (1928) shows, like his close colleague Glaspell's *Suppressed Desires*, direct engagement with Freud's ideas, experimenting with how theatre could express characters' inner lives: characters speak directly to the audience, with others frozen on stage while they reveal their private thoughts in lengthy, revealing asides. O'Neill's experimentation continued in *Mourning Becomes Electra* (1931), a modern recreation of the Oresteia set in the Deep South during the American Civil War and lasting a full nine hours. Like Shaw in *Back to Methuselah* (1920), O'Neill redefined the standard length of a play and gave a different meaning to 'epic', built more on Greek mythology than Marxist theory. Yet despite all of these innovations, O'Neill is often remembered as the playwright of the poisonous family secret.

A playwright who serves as a corrective to Nightingale's dismissal of modern American 'diaper drama' is Lillian Hellman. She seems to find the balance between dark, domestic secrets in claustrophobically enclosed and stifling communities—families, schools—and their wider political implications. She explores how people live when they seem fundamentally at odds with the society around them. And she achieved remarkable success with her hard-hitting dramas *The Little Foxes* (1939) and *The Children's Hour* (1934).

The Children's Hour shows the spiralling impact of a lie that a vengeful student at a girls' boarding school tells about the headmistresses, Martha and Karen, that they are lesbians having an affair. Most of the students are pulled out of the school by their homophobic parents, the women lose their case in court, their school closes down, and when Martha realizes that she is indeed sexually attracted to Karen but Karen rejects her, she commits suicide. Hellman excoriates a society that will not allow for individuality, that pressures people to conform to narrow norms, and she looks outwards for the sources of blame instead of inwards to character flaws or family weaknesses.

Social oppression was often legally as well as culturally enforced, for example in Britain where homosexuality only began to be decriminalized in 1967, and playwrights had to find ways of submerging or cloaking their criticisms or have their work censored or banned. Noel Coward and Terence Rattigan, whose careers began in this period, became particularly adept at this Wildean subterfuge. Like artists and writers everywhere in this era of political violence, playwrights often suffered for their work. Both Meyerhold and Lorca were executed, Josef Čapek died at the Bergen-Belsen concentration camp in 1945, and Flanagan Davis, Brecht, Arthur Miller, and many fellow theatre artists fell victim to the 'red scare' led by Senator Joseph McCarthy and the HUAC.

Chapter 4
Salesmen, southerners, anger, and ennui

The 1940s and 1950s encompass some of the most famous events in modern drama: the staging of Tennessee Williams' *A Streetcar Named Desire* (1947) and Arthur Miller's *Death of a Salesman* (1949), attaining a new kind of tragedy and a particularly American brand of realism; and the London premieres of Beckett's *Waiting for Godot* (1955; written in French in 1948–9 and first produced in French as *En attendant Godot* in Paris in 1953) and John Osborne's *Look Back in Anger* (1956)—introducing on the one hand the 'theatre of the absurd' and on the other hand a new linguistic and emotional brutality, inaugurating an era of 'kitchen sink' realism in the theatre. In radically different ways these various strains of drama expanded the subject matter of plays as well as their formal and linguistic properties; in particular, they changed the way language (and silence) worked on stage. This is the main area of overlap among the disparate dramatic forms explored in this chapter.

Directly or indirectly, many of the plays in this period were responses to World War II and its aftermath, the Cold War. Playwrights express despair at the cost in human lives and the destruction of cities across Europe and Asia; horror at the reality of the Holocaust and the introduction of weapons of mass destruction; yet also cautious optimism at the prospect of economic recovery and the signs of prosperity, including in Britain a new set of sweeping reforms that included universal health care and education. Playwrights become even bolder in their gestures than in previous periods in experimenting with new forms, language, and themes. In particular, plays reach new levels of violence, rethink the meaning of tragedy, and show a marked impatience with propriety and reticence. It is as if the war unleashed revolutionary forces in the theatre, none more pronounced than the continued attack on the audience and the attempts to break down the 'fourth wall' it represented.

American realism

Some of the most famous and enduring modern dramas came from America in these decades, starting in the mid-1940s: plays like Tennessee Williams' *The Glass Menagerie* (1944) and *A Streetcar Named Desire* (1947) and Arthur Miller's *All My Sons* (1947) and *Death of a Salesman* (1949). But American drama diverged sharply from that in Britain in this period. Realism still dominated the American stage, reinforced by the rise of Method acting and by the popularity of Hollywood film versions of plays that erase the non-realistic elements of the original dramas in favour of an all-encompassing naturalism.

Method acting, made famous by actors like Marlon Brando, was an American version of Stanislavski's theories that emphasized complete immersion of the actor in the role and demanded a new grittiness to both the staging and the acting. 'The Method' combined subtly nuanced characterization with social awareness and helped to bring American drama into the world repertoire. Plays explored the psyche of the American character, and criticized US ideals. The focus on the individual and the family discussed at the end of Chapter 3 as a significant development in modern drama, particularly in America, was linked directly to the Method—a reminder that plays are often shaped by the theatrical conditions of their times *more* than they shape such conditions. It wouldn't have been possible for O'Neill, Miller, or Williams to write such psychologically penetrating characters if it hadn't been for Method acting. O'Neill's reputation had languished until his autobiographical play *Long Day's Journey into Night* (written in 1941) was staged by Jose Quintero in 1956 so searingly and powerfully through this new kind of acting.

Like Thornton Wilder, Tennessee Williams employed anti-realistic techniques in many of his plays that were aimed at disrupting the processes of identification and catharsis so dominant in contemporary theatre. Williams was one of Piscator's students at the Dramatic Workshop in New York. Because of their total erasure in the process of being made into Hollywood blockbusters, it is easy to overlook the presence of epic theatre techniques in Williams' plays. But they are there, with such strength that a play like *The Glass Menagerie* (1944) reads like a textbook example of epic drama, with its use of metatheatre as Tom restages scenes from his family life for us, with placards announcing the contents of each scene, Tom as the framing narrator, screen projections with pithy sayings, and simple but suggestive use of scaffolding (the fire escape on which Tom perches to smoke and tell his story). At key moments in the play, just when the audience might get swept up in emotional identification with the characters, legends appear on the screen that comment ironically, even sarcastically, on the action: 'Not Jim!', 'The Opening of a Door!', or simply 'Terror!' Shortly before his death in 2005 Arthur Miller recalled the impact of *The Glass Menagerie* when he saw it on its opening in New York in 1944. The play was so unusual in its lyricism, it was 'like stumbling on a flower in a junkyard, a triumph of fragility, a play utterly at odds with standard Broadway fare'.

With *A Streetcar Named Desire*, Williams brought these qualities to bear even more powerfully through his portrayal of fading Southern belle Blanche DuBois arriving in a run-down house in New Orleans to stay indefinitely with her sister Stella, married to the earthy Stanley Kowalski and expecting their first baby. Relaying the plot is easy, but it doesn't capture Williams' unique theatricality—at once realistic yet expressionist and poetic—because most of these qualities are in the stage directions, which can easily get ignored.

For example, music plays a vital role throughout the play, expressing the characters' inner states as well as setting the jazz and blues tone of New Orleans. The final moments of the play call for 'the swelling music of the "blue piano" and the muted trumpet' that have haunted the play from the beginning. And, just as O'Neill's *The Emperor Jones* had used African drumming expressionistically to evoke the human heartbeat, in *Streetcar* we hear 'inhuman cries and noises' in the background conveying Blanche's disturbed state of mind.

In fact, Williams experimented with theatrical form throughout his career. *Camino Real* (1953) shows a side of Williams that people rarely see or even know about, so dominant is his image as a realistic playwright. The vast canvas of this sprawling theatrical work combines dream sequences, transhistorical settings, and intertextuality (the characters include a range of figures from world literature, such as Don Quixote and Sancho Panza, Lord Byron, Casanova, the Lady of the Camellias, the Hunchback of Notre Dame). In 1970, the theatre critic Clive Barnes declared it Williams' 'best play', 'torn out of a human soul, a tale told by an idiot signifying a great deal of suffering and a great deal of gallantry'.

But Williams is best known now for his portraits of women at extremes: Amanda in *Glass Menagerie*, Blanche DuBois in *Streetcar*, Maggie in *Cat on a Hot Tin Roof* (1955). These female characters are pushed to the edge by circumstances hostile to them and they have to adapt or be crushed. Maggie, who desperately wants a child and a 'normal' marriage, has to face the fact that her husband Brick is a closet homosexual. The cost of keeping this secret from everyone is clear from the first moments of the play, in which he drinks steadily and barely speaks. Big Daddy, Brick's father, confronts him with his sexuality: 'this disgust with mendacity is disgust with yourself', because he won't admit the truth and accept his own nature. The effects of deceit—both lying to others and lying to oneself—are at the centre of this play, echoing Hellman's concerns in *The Children's Hour*. The word 'mendacity' is the play's keynote, repeated throughout in different contexts as the family members confront each other in increasingly searing scenes of recrimination.

The play's strong language and emotionally wrenching family confrontations, exposing the lies at the heart of spousal and filial relationships, set a key precedent that younger playwrights like Edward Albee followed. In his first play, *The Zoo Story* (1959), a young drifter named Jerry tries to make friends with the stolid and bourgeois Peter, reading on a bench in Central Park. Jerry's friendliness becomes increasingly insistent as the stories he tells convey the need for emotional connection in an indifferent and often cruel world; eventually, out of the blue, the play turns violent as he impales himself on a knife he has forced Peter to hold.

In his next play, Albee shows the obverse: rather than a meeting of strangers, *Who's Afraid of Virginia Woolf?* (1962) hinges on a meeting of two married couples, the older George and Martha and the younger Nick and Honey, connected through work as George and Nick are colleagues in the same department at a college in New England. Albee goes even further than Williams in dramatizing the ultimately destructive effect of family life built around self-deceit, lying, and illusion, the cost of maintaining an external image of happiness when the core is rotten.

Martha and George, named for the iconic American president George Washington and his wife (the founding family), take Nick and Honey through a long, alcohol-soaked night during which the couples' lives unravel. In the first act, called 'Fun and Games', Nick and Honey watch as George and Martha's bickering turns into increasingly barbed banter that reveals their mutual hatred. Then the younger couple gets drawn into these verbal games. Slowly, the audience learns that the pressure on the women to conform to the idealized American family has led to the concoction of imaginary children: Honey has a 'false pregnancy', while Martha has invented a son for her and George, a shared delusion that he has agreed to go along with but that he will destroy on this night in the final act of the play, called 'Exorcism'.

For both Albee and Williams, the pressure to conform to a heterosexual lifestyle built around the nuclear family is particularly troubling in its utter repression of otherness, of any departure from that norm. When Martha loses her imaginary son, as George announces that he has been killed in a car accident, she feels her loss as a Greek heroine would feel hers, grieving and devastated, a tragic figure. Albee signals that this death has been redemptive. He revisits this concept in much of his work, most recently in *The Goat; or, Who is Sylvia?* Common to these and other American playwrights is a sense that, far from disappearing or becoming outmoded in the modern world, the genre of tragedy has new meaning and new forms.

A new model of tragedy

In fact, tragedy was enjoying a major revival and reimagining in this period. In his plays as well as his essays, Arthur Miller articulated a new theory of tragedy, defending his controversial depiction of an ordinary salesman as a tragic hero by saying that it is not about status: a grocer can be a tragic hero just as a king can. Like Ibsen's 'Notes to the Modern Tragedy' for *A Doll's House*, Miller's essay 'Tragedy and the Common Man' (1949) is a manifesto for a new vision of tragedy. It's all about the intensity of the commitment the character has to his or her goal, not the goal itself. 'I think the tragic feeling is evoked in us when we are in the presence of a character who is ready to lay down his life, if need be, to secure one thing—his sense of personal dignity.'

Miller defined tragedy as emanating from indignation, 'the fateful wound' that leads to a spiralling of events as the individual struggles to 'gain his "rightful" position in his society'. For Miller, the defining aspect of the modern tragic 'hero' is not the Aristotelian 'fatal flaw' but the total commitment to his chosen course of action, regardless of how wrong it might be. It is, as he would say repeatedly, 'man's total compulsion to evaluate himself justly'. His argument is that these feelings of total compulsion and commitment are not the province of the aristocratic class, but 'the heart and spirit of the average man'. That is what is modern. Willy Loman may be pursuing entirely the wrong course of action from our point of view, but that is not the issue: it is his commitment to that course that matters, and that makes him tragic in these new terms. His world begins to crumble from the moment he realizes how big a gap there is between his idea of himself and the idea others have of him. The play thus explores 'the underlying fear of being displaced, the disaster inherent in being torn away from our chosen image of what and who we are in this world'. Miller does suggest, paradoxically, a note of optimism hidden in all tragedy. 'The plays we revere, century after century, are the tragedies. In them, and in them alone, lies the belief—optimistic, if you will, in the perfectibility of man.'

Miller put this new tragic vision into his plays *All My Sons* (1947) and *Death of a Salesman* (1949). The latter has an undisputed place at the top of the list of world dramas, enduringly popular in China and indeed all over the world (most recently in Abu Dhabi). But Miller's elements of non-realism in the play are often overlooked. His 'realism', like Williams', has pronounced non-realistic elements designed to disrupt the seemingly stable, straightforward narrative of Willy's experiences. He intersperses realistic scenes in Willy's home (a set that is supposed to evoke 'the inside of his head', rather than just a house, as the upper windows are eyes and the door is the mouth) with 'time-bends', which are similar to flashbacks; the characters move seamlessly in and out of these temporal zones, in and out of Willy's memory, all within a seemingly realistic framework. He called the play a 'memory play', similar to Williams' concept in *Glass Menagerie*.

Anger and all that

Most of the plays discussed in this chapter so far had their successes on Broadway. During this period, there wasn't much alternative in the US; there was not yet much regional theatre, and no off-Broadway. This is very different from Britain, where regional theatres had been developing for years, and where the West End was beginning to branch out and see much greater variety of theatres. In fact, individual theatres played a key role in housing, and often shaping, the drama of this period in Britain.

Driven by post-war idealism, the Old Vic led the campaign for a national theatre—a campaign whose roots stretched back decades to around 1900—by showing what a permanent company playing in repertory could achieve. The Old Vic's key practitioners were Michael St Denis (nephew of Jacques Copeau), who founded the pioneering London Theatre Studio in 1936; George Devine, who had worked with St Denis and later helped found and direct the English Stage Company, housed at the Royal Court Theatre; and director Glen Byam Shaw. These men all worked at the Old Vic's newly created Theatre Centre, which encompassed an experimental theatre that launched in 1946.

The Royal Court Theatre opened in 1955/6 with productions under George Devine and the English Stage Company; the third of these, *Look Back in Anger* (1956), initiated a new phase in British drama that was all about taking risks, tearing down social barriers, and being outspoken on a stage that was, after all, still government censored. At this time, the grand older generation of playwrights, Noel Coward, Terence Rattigan, and J.B. Priestley, were still going strong; *Look Back in Anger* seemed fresh and invigorating compared to the well-made plays generally on offer, and legend has it that the play revolutionized British drama almost overnight.

Yet a number of myths surround *Look Back in Anger*. For one thing, it only became a hit when a short excerpt of it was shown on TV months after its rather lacklustre premiere, at a time that happened to coincide with the national political drama known as the Suez Crisis, which threw Britain's status as an empire into question and revealed its crumbling international power. In addition, the label 'angry young man' came about by accident, when Osborne's publicity manager in an interview just threw it out on the spur of the moment. That label has proven as indelible as 'theatre of the absurd', and with similar complications and inaccuracies. What does the white, middle-class Jimmy Porter have to be so angry about? There is no reason why this well-educated young man should be running a sweet stall and ranting about social injustice at a time when Britain's unemployment rate was a mere 1.3 per cent. Osborne gives us no good reason for this choice of occupation; nor does he seem to question sticking Alison, Jimmy's long-suffering wife, behind an ironing board for most of the play, and having Jimmy not just condone but actually celebrate the fact that she has a miscarriage because she will finally 'feel' something.

Despite its extraordinary misogyny and masochism *Look Back in Anger* still gets celebrated for its revolutionary impact. Yet as a piece of theatre, it does nothing new whatsoever: structurally, it harks back to the 19th-century 'well-made' play, and one full of weaknesses at that. Only in the dialogue, with its unprecedented venting of spleen, does the play lay some claim to innovation.

This was not lost on Osborne's contemporaries. Shelagh Delaney's *A Taste of Honey* (1958) came out of a dissatisfaction with the world view that *Look Back in Anger* represented: white, male, and middle class. In place of Jimmy Porter angrily vilifying 'society' from his comfortable bedsit, reading the newspaper while his wife does the chores, Delaney presents the young working-class girl Jo and her mother Helen living in a tiny flat in Salford. Jo's lover Jimmy is a black sailor who returns to sea, leaving Jo pregnant and alone. She then moves in with Geoffrey, a homosexual friend who becomes a surrogate father. Far from showing the world according to the educated white male, Delaney packs issues of class, race, gender, and sexuality into her play at a time when homosexuality was still illegal, class prejudice was rife, and women and minorities struggled to find fair treatment in society as well as full representation on the stage.

No more masterpieces

As the foregoing discussion shows, the core of theatre was still realism, with its family constellations and domestic settings. This was counterbalanced by several key developments: 'happenings', Artaud's 'theatre of cruelty', and absurdism, new flanks in the ongoing attack on realism that began in earnest with Brecht.

'Happenings' (a term coined by Allan Kaprow) were early forms of performance art and devised theatre, drawing on the visual arts and music and freeing the theatrical event from the primacy of the text; instead, multidisciplinarity, environment, and incident became key elements. The fundamental aim of happenings is to erase the boundary between the work of art and its audience. They flourished in the 1960s under such leading figures as the Polish director Tadeusz Kantor, Jean-Jacques Lebel in France, and the Bread and Puppet Theatre in New York (later Vermont).

Antonin Artaud's *The Theatre and its Double* was first translated into English in 1958 (though begun as far back as the 1920s and published in France in 1938). This little book had an extraordinary impact on 20th-century theatre, despite the lack of scripts that actually implement the ideas in it—perhaps because, as many feel, they are so extreme as to be unstageable.

Like Pirandello, Piscator, Meyerhold, and Brecht, Artaud rebelled against the idea of theatre as a showpiece of realistic scenes of life. He coined the term 'theatre of cruelty' to describe his aims of a 'total theatre' that would be all-consuming and overwhelming, like a ritual or a festival blurring the line between participants and observers, theatre and life. He envisioned this total theatre involving all aspects of sensory perception: vision, smell, taste, hearing, touch, sound. The key element is that this theatrical experience should be direct and unmediated; the audience should be immersed in it, not seeing a representation but feeling its direct presence.

A related idea is theatre as 'plague': like a disease, theatre should convey its ideas through the body, from person to person, altering each body it infected. Artaud also wanted to get rid of 'masterpieces'—classic plays that have become museum pieces of the theatre. Such concepts as 'plague' and 'cruelty' have powerfully inspired a host of subsequent playwrights and directors. And, like many other theatre practitioners in modern drama, Artaud was directly influenced by non-Western theatre practice—Balinese puppet theatre, stylized gestures, and scenarios rather than scripted and dialogue-led scenes.

Theatre of the absurd

Absurdist theatre brought existentialist philosophy on to the stage. 'Absurd' does not carry its more modern connotation of 'ridiculous', 'silly', or 'unbelievable' as when we dismiss something as 'absurd' because it is implausible. Instead, it has its roots in Camus' essay 'The Myth of Sisyphus' (1942), in which 'absurd' is used to signify the modern condition of living in a world that seems meaningless, in which humans are mere puppets at the mercy of invisible external forces.

Absurdist plays, as Esslin explained in his seminal book *The Theatre of the Absurd* (1961), show that the ways we have devised to make sense of our lives and our world—concepts like order, linear causality, and reason—are really just fictions imposed on a reality whose meaning will always elude us. In a way, this is similar to Pirandello's philosophy: humans construct masks and labels that we believe are our identities (doctor, lawyer, king, wife, daughter, etc.) just to create a sense of fixity and order in a chaotic, fluid world.

Audiences of absurdist plays do not get privileged knowledge that is hidden from the characters (dramatic irony), as in many realist dramas. We are in the dark about causes of situations and reasons for behaviour as much as the characters are. We don't know who Godot is or why he isn't coming. We have no idea why Lucky spews language like vomit, or why chairs mysteriously appear on stage in *The Chairs*. In addition, absurdist plays have certain features in common: they are tragic-comic hybrids; they feature characters stuck in hopeless situations, doing the same things over and over again, yet with no point or goal to be realized; they have cyclical plots; they sometimes use horror and exaggeration, and the dialogue contains puns, nonsensical or unexplained allusions, and intertexual references. The audience has to interpret such linguistic signs, making meaning where it can.

Esslin identified four main playwrights of the absurd: Samuel Beckett, Arthur Adamov, Eugene Ionesco, and Jean Genet. Others include Anouilh, Pinter, Dürrenmatt, early Stoppard, and (to some extent) Albee. All have their roots in earlier experiments on stage such as Jarry's *Ubu Roi* and Dada and surrealist theatre, with their nonsensical situations that remain unexplained to audience and characters alike, their incongruous juxtapositions, and their grotesque exaggeration.

Sartre in particular, like Camus, was specifically excluded from the movement by Esslin and others, as working from a related philosophical base but creating a very different kind of theatre in existentialist plays like *Huis Clos* (*No Exit*, 1944). In this play, three dead people are trapped in an ordinary, bourgeois living room that turns out to be Hell, and they are kept there by a mysterious eyelid-less valet. Realizing that they have been put there to torture each other mentally for all eternity, they confess their past crimes in the hope of easing the situation—but, if anything, things get worse and they end up senselessly stabbing themselves and each other, which has no effect since they are already dead. This makes the characters burst into hysterical laughter; the play ends inconclusively with the line 'well, let's go on', which Beckett's *Waiting for Godot* echoes a decade later: 'Let's go. (*They do not move.*)' Beckett provides a similar scenario in his purgatorial play *Play* (1963), but instead of the recognizably bourgeois setting that Sartre had given, Beckett puts his three characters into giant urns, with just their heads protruding, which makes their bickering dialogue about their love affairs all the more banal, pointless, and incongruous.

Stasis, lack of resolution, lack of agency, vague and hostile external forces—these qualities characterize many of the situations in absurdist plays. In Ionesco's *The Chairs* (1952), a couple find themselves mysteriously surrounded by an increasing number of chairs that appear out of nowhere and with no explanation. In Beckett's *Act Without Words I* (1956), a man in a desert is manipulated by an unseen force that seems to taunt and tantalize him, flinging him on and off stage, presenting a carafe of water that he tries in vain to reach, and perplexing him with other strange objects like cubes, scissors, and a lasso. This unseen force seems very close as it whistles commandingly at moments. Although such situations may seem to make no sense, these plays are not meaningless or without action: meaning resides in the characters' struggle to understand their condition.

This can be directly linked to the period—it is no coincidence that such plays begin to appear in the mid-1940s, reflecting a despair that after two devastating world wars and the Holocaust, what meaning is left? They are also deeply connected to existentialist philosophy. If we are mere specks in a void without meaning, we have to *create* meaning, since it is not given. This is the missing piece of the picture often painted of absurdism in definitions that focus on its inherent meaninglessness and the idea that nothing happens. In fact, throughout the plays of the absurd, we can see constant instances of characters creating meaning through language and indeed even through silences, which are not voids but take on semantic weight in this kind of drama.

The idea that no one (i.e. God) is at the helm giving meaning to life, but that we have to make it ourselves, is actually tremendously liberating even if it is also scary. Informed that there is 'no more nature' outside, perhaps because of some nuclear apocalypse (Beckett doesn't tell us), Hamm in *Endgame* (1957) insists that nature still carries on: 'But we breathe, we change! We lose our hair, our teeth! Our bloom! Our ideals!' In contrast to his defeatist partner/servant Clov, who passively accepts that 'something is taking its course', the blind Hamm actively creates meaning by reciting stories, quotations from Shakespeare and the Bible, snatches of songs, even just interesting words ('accursed progenitor!').

Ionesco once said of Beckett that he expressed a 'very naked reality' through 'the apparent dislocation of language'. That naked reality was the failure of humans to overcome the absurdity of existence; our failure to know and to do, our constant sense of impoverishment, exile, and loss. Beckett, who won the Nobel Prize in Literature in 1970, was inspired by the comic traditions of vaudeville, music hall, and silent film. The tramps in *Waiting for Godot*, the extended joke-telling of *Endgame* (Figure 6), the slapstick routines in many of his plays, remind us of Charlie Chaplin, the Keystone Cops, Buster Keaton, the Marx Brothers, and Laurel and Hardy—combining physical comedy and farcical situations with an essentially barren, diminished environment, so devoid of basic physical comforts that the characters fall back on language as a means of spiritual sustenance and existential

6. 'Nothing is funnier than unhappiness, I grant you that': parents in ashcans in Samuel Beckett's *Endgame*, in a 2009 production at the Duchess Theatre, London, directed by Simon McBurney; with Tom Hickey as Nagg and Miriam Margolyes as Nell.

affirmation. A joke isn't just entertainment or a way of passing the time; 'I *talk*, therefore I am' might well be the motto of the absurd, even while it also emphasizes mime and silence.

Edward Albee is often described as part of the second wave of absurdist playwrights, which amused and irritated him. Albee asked 'which theatre is the absurd one?' in a famous essay of that title, implying that it is Broadway, and not the so-called absurdists, that is the nonsensical theatre, with its soaring ticket prices, narrowness of audiences and directors alike, and complete dominance of theatre in America, for example showing itself impervious to influences that were invigorating theatre elsewhere such as Brecht and Artaud.

Brecht's Berliner Ensemble visited London in 1956 and inaugurated a long line of influence on British drama, from Joan Littlewood, Edward Bond, and Ewan MacColl through Caryl Churchill, Howard Brenton, David Hare, Trevor Griffiths, and

John McGrath. Brecht also deeply influenced playwrights and directors across Europe including Dario Fo, Augusto Boal, Peter Brook, Peter Weiss, and Heiner Müller.

Some of Brecht's most significant plays reached worldwide audiences during these decades, and his published writings on theatre become enshrined in John Willett's *Brecht on Theatre* (1957). *Mr Puntila and His Man Matti* (1940/8); *The Good Person of Szechwan* (1939–42/1943); *The Resistible Rise of Arturo Ui* (1941/58); *The Caucasian Chalk Circle* (1943–5/1948); his essay 'A Short Organon for the Theatre', published 1949; these all stem from this period, at a time when the other emerging theatrical voice that would leave an equally powerful legacy was that of Beckett, whose *Waiting for Godot* seemed to lie at the other end of the ever-widening dramatic spectrum. Two tramps waiting in a barren landscape for a character who never came; compared to Brecht's plays, there didn't seem to be an obvious structure, social message, or overall point.

Around 1960, then, theatre seems to become polarized into distinct, opposing camps: Brechtian versus Beckettian, political versus absurdist. These kinds of absolute positions distort the truth of the matter, which is that there is some blurring of borders and thematic overlap. But they come about through highly public debates waged among prominent critics and playwrights: Eugene Ionesco versus Kenneth Tynan, Edward Bond taking a stance against 'theatre of the absurd', Joe Orton criticizing mainstream theatregoers ('Aunt Edna'). The point is that theatre really mattered, just as the *Playboy* riots and other outbursts in theatres in previous decades had shown.

Poetic plays and radio drama

But did all theatre matter? Leading poets like T.S. Eliot, W.H. Auden, and Christopher Isherwood felt that the gritty settings and everyday language of modern plays had crowded out the poetry, and they attempted to give modern verse drama renewed life on the stage in the 1930s and 1940s. Eliot's *The Family Reunion*

(1939) and *The Cocktail Party* (1949) follow on from Auden and Isherwood's *The Dog Beneath the Skin* (1935) and *The Ascent of F6* (1937). Auden and Isherwood's plays combined whimsical, playful qualities with a serious social message; they have much in common with Brecht's theatre, despite their more poetic inclinations. Eliot's verse drama is entirely different. He attempts to fuse Greek mythology and drama with modern realistic settings and characters speaking in verse (along similar lines to O'Neill's use of Greek myth described in Chapter 3)—not exactly standard West End or Broadway fare, and not a success.

This latter development is related to the rise of radio plays in this period, well suited to poetic drama. As Louis MacNeice observed of his own radio play *The Dark Tower* (1946), there was no 'clear moral or message', it had 'the solidity of a dream', and it benefited from the exclusively aural form because its inherent 'stream of consciousness...subordinat[ed] analysis to synthesis' and appealed to 'more primitive elements' in its audience. The most famous radio play remains Dylan Thomas's *Under Milk Wood* (1953), a 'play for voices' that movingly captured life in a fictional Welsh village through vividly created and vocally differentiated characters.

Radio drama at its best was free of 'the physical limitations of the stage, and the crudity of visual symbolism', and it appealed 'directly to the ear and the imagination', allowing for 'subjective lyricism' that was helpful to the revival of poetic drama. Beckett too was attracted to radio drama; for example, he wrote *All that Fall* (1956), a one-act radio play that aired in 1957, at the request of the BBC. As the ageing and lame Mrs Rooney trudges along a country road to meet her husband at the train station, she talks to people she meets and we hear the sounds of a horse, a wagon, a car, and then a train, a soundscape that conveys the evolution of human transportation. For a playwright famous for his linguistic minimalism the play is a revelation, and shows how, far from being impoverished by the lack of a visual dimension, the radio form concentrates the listener's mind and enhances language and sound.

Chapter 5
Absurdism, protest, and commitment

The alleged 'anger' that Osborne had famously pointed to pales by comparison with the rage that comes to define, and fuel, much of the drama of the 1960s and beyond—and instead of anger among the characters, it is directed at the audience. It is a post-war rage stemming from many sources: the Vietnam War, the Cold War, a feeling of betrayal by government and politicians, the Civil Rights Movement, Black Power, gay rights, feminism, the growing gap between rich and poor, ethnic oppression. The decades 1960–80 witnessed a seismic shift in modern drama, signalled by these lines from Handke:

> You will see no spectacle.
> Your curiosity will not be satisfied.
> You will see no play.
> Peter Handke, *Offending the Audience* (1966), trans. Michael Roloff
> (Act 1)

It's all about denying the audience what it expects of a play, provoking it out of real or perceived complacency, startling and offending it. We have seen that this streak of provocation runs through much of modern drama before this period—think of *Ubu Roi*'s 'Merdre!', Pirandello's unsettling use of metatheatre, or Brecht's *Verfremdungseffekt*—but what accounts for the new level of hostility? Was post-war society getting too materialistic and comfortable, masking the injustices within society, such as ongoing racism, homophobia, and misogyny? And had society ever really come to terms with the events of the war—the Holocaust, the use of atomic weapons—or had it just turned its back and preferred to forget?

Playwrights in these decades seek to remind the audience constantly of its conscience. They do so partly by exploding conventions of theatre, sweeping away old forms and inventing new ones. Their provocation becomes more extreme, the challenges to audience sensibilities more overt and transgressive. It's as if playwrights want to traumatize audiences, not just make them momentarily uncomfortable. And this doesn't always happen by directly addressing the audience, even though that is a key element of theatre at this time (Handke's play being a prime example); the shock and challenge to the audience also comes in realistic plays, with the audience still playing the part of the fourth wall. In Peter Shaffer's *Equus* (1973), a psychiatrist tries to understand why a teenage boy finds sexual gratification by blinding horses. In Edward Bond's *Saved* (1965), the audience watches in horror as a group of teenagers stones a baby to death in its pram; our inability to do anything about it except watch is part of the play's exploration of violence in contemporary society. Even worse, the character that seemed most sympathetic turns out to have been watching the whole event from behind a tree.

Whether we are directly implicated or silently ignored, *we* are the focus of these plays; the idea is to make us face the problems and injustices of society and acknowledge that we are complicit in them. 'Society is usually based on injustice or expediency,' writes Bond, 'but art is the expression of moral sanity.' His work and that of many other dramatists of this time revolves around this vision of art. It is not, in an Aristotelian sense, an art that purges the audience of its violence by forcing us to face this impulse in ourselves, because that would mean we could just leave the theatre and forget what we had seen. Rather, a confrontation happens in the theatre that is so powerful that you leave changed in a fundamental way. This would characterize the plays of Sarah Kane, whose 1995 *Blasted* imprints itself on the spectator's mind through hitherto unimaginable violence, a direct link to Artaud's theatre of cruelty. Bond was one of the brave voices that supported her play in the face of almost universal condemnation.

There have been many other significant ways of capturing and addressing the post-war condition in modern theatre. Leading Hungarian playwright István Örkény developed a 'grotesque' theatre that combines elements such as absurdism, epic, and allegory, as in *Stevie in the Bloodstorm* (1969), showing a contemporary Hungarian Everyman (played by four actors) set in a grotesque panoramic sweep of modern history. The plays that made him internationally recognized, *The Tóth Family* (1967) and *Catsplay* (1971), likewise, though in radically different ways, examine the concept of national character and the master–slave dynamic.

Robert Wilson has been working with experimental theatre since the 1960s and is one of its foremost practitioners, drawing on all the possible elements of performance to create original productions as well as new stagings of classic works. Like Adolphe Appia before him, Wilson believes that light is the most important part of theatre. Yet there is also language, silence, music, dance, movement, and the visual arts; all of these recombine in Wilson's work in powerful ways, for example in his collaboration with Philip Glass on *Einstein on the Beach* (1976) and his productions in the 1990s of Gertrude Stein's difficult and obscure works for the stage. Like his contemporaries Tadeusz Kantor and the composer John Cage, Wilson has helped to redefine theatre and performance fundamentally, and has influenced the next generation of experimental practitioners like the prolific and wide-ranging Italian director Romeo Castellucci.

Is violence *funny*?

Bond takes violence to a new and unprecedented level in *Saved* (1965) and *Early Morning* (1968), plays that helped to bring about the end of theatrical censorship in England. Meanwhile, Joe Orton completely reinvented farce during his tragically brief career in the 1960s, generating a new brand of 'black comedy' that continues to develop today through playwrights like Martin McDonagh.

Orton's *Entertaining Mr Sloane* (1964) was endorsed by none other than playwright Terence Rattigan whose financial and written support ensured the play's success through transferral to Wyndham's Theatre in the West End (though it flopped in New York the following year), and Orton's next performed play was *Loot* (1965), a hilarious black farce set in a funeral parlour and echoed by Jez Butterworth's *Mojo* decades later (a similarly farcical plot with a dead parent's body having to be unceremoniously hidden). *Loot* ran for over 300 performances at the Criterion Theatre, London, in 1966, and won several awards, but it flopped on Broadway in 1968. The gulf between American and British audiences with regard to what was tolerated in the theatre was deep. Orton's final full-length play, *What the Butler Saw*, premiered in the West End in 1969, after Orton's death. His legacy to subsequent drama includes reinventing farce and opening up taboo areas such as sex and violence through black humour.

Sex and violence also permeate the Swiss playwright Friedrich Dürrenmatt's *The Physicists* (1961; premiere 1962). Three scientists posing as psychiatric patients who believe they are famous physicists—Newton, Möbius, and Einstein—strangle their attractive young nurses, but are eventually subject to the will of the tyrannical Doctor von Zahnd, head of the asylum, who has tricked the men into revealing their scientific secrets so that she may eventually become the most powerful woman on earth. The serious subject matter and tragic ending are tempered and complicated by the formally innovative use of pastiche, transhistorical characters and transtemporal settings, and parody of thriller/noir detective fiction and films, and the play is put in a Cold War context with specific hostility to science and its repercussions. Its central question—whether we can unknow what we know—runs through many 'science plays' right to the present day.

Absurdism and politics

Dürrenmatt is often categorized as an absurdist playwright, highlighting the ways in which absurdism continued to develop in the 1960s–1980s, taking in new playwrights who subtly change its scope and direction. Absurdism was brought directly to bear on specific oppressive political regimes across the world, as in the work of Czech playwright, dissident activist, and later President of the Czech Republic Václav Havel (notably his play *The Garden Party*, 1963), Argentinian writer Griselda Gambaro, and German playwright Heiner Müller.

Gambaro is Argentina's leading playwright. Her most famous plays were written from the 1960s onwards and tackle political oppression, criticizing her country's history of military brutality and government-sponsored terrorism. Like many of her works, her play *Information for Foreigners: A Chronicle in Twenty Scenes* (1973) shows the world gone mad, a place in which killing and torture are just part of everyday existence. 'Nothing more was ever known' is one of the key lines in the play, referring to the 'disappeared'—the hundreds of thousands of murdered and/or imprisoned civilians under the military governments during the 1970s and 1980s.

The play doesn't just point the finger at politicians, however. It suggests that the seemingly innocent onlooker is culpable by being complicit and pliant in the face of authority. The fourth scene recreates the notorious experiments conducted by psychologist Stanley Milgram at Yale University in 1961 in which participants were ordered to administer a series of increasingly strong electric shocks to unseen but heard subjects; even in the face of evident agony (simulated, though they did not know this), and in conflict with their own conscience, the participants kept following the orders of the scientists in charge. These controversial experiments suggested that people will go to extreme lengths, even killing others, to carry out orders given by those in authority. Milgram's experiments coincided with the trial of Nazi war criminal Adolf Eichmann in Israel, and raised questions not just about how authority figures can do monstrous things but about the mysterious forces within ordinary people that cause them to comply with wrongdoing even though they know better.

Gambaro's play takes the audience through many scenarios in different styles, united by the common idea of implicating the audience even while it is 'just' watching the action. 'Theatre is a risky business!' shouts the Guide who takes the audience through the scenes and offers dry, sarcastic commentary. On many levels, the play highlights the notion of the audience as itself performing a role.

Indeed, the overtly political theatre that emerges all over the world in these decades often explicitly invokes its own genre as its main metaphor. Heiner Müller spent most of his career using the 'risky business of theatre' to question the East German government, and became the most important German-language playwright since Brecht. *Hamletmachine* (1977) is, like Gambaro's *Information for Foreigners*, a loosely connected series of scenes, and has become one of the most highly regarded postmodern plays—that is, fragmentary, disjointed plays that fuse different styles and avoid linear, causal development and psychological characters, seeming more like a pastiche than an integrated, organic whole and constantly reminding the audience of theatre's illusion and role-playing.

In act one of *Hamletmachine*, The Actor Playing Hamlet says to the audience: 'I'm not Hamlet. I don't take part any more. My words have nothing to tell me anymore. My thoughts suck the blood out of the images. My drama doesn't happen anymore. Behind me the set is put up.' Is this what has happened, the play seems to be asking, to the promise of socialism in Europe, to the very idea of revolution in the modern world? Are political movements mere sets and backdrops, without substance and meaning?

History also comes in for a drubbing at the hands of directors like Joan Littlewood, whose *Oh! What a Lovely War* (1963) fused Brechtian operatic, dramatic, and musical techniques with British theatrical traditions drawn from cabaret and vaudeville (cross-dressing, drag queen showpiece, war songs) to re-examine the forces that led to World War I and cast a scathing eye on the glorification of war in general. Like Littlewood's play, John McGrath's *The Cheviot, the Stag, and the Black, Black Oil* (1973), presented by his company 7:84 all over Scotland in community centres, churches, and other local venues, drew on music hall and Brechtian theatre to explore Scottish history, but went further by adapting the text to each new locality in which they performed, and thus spoke directly to its audiences' specific concerns. These are both early examples of devised theatre, a vital current of drama that began in the 1960s and 1970s and which flourishes in new incarnations today, as I discuss in Chapter 6.

Other playwrights during the period 1960–80 turned their backs on history and politics, preferring to explore the internal landscape of the mind and the inscrutable forces that determine who we are.

The audience must do the work

Stoppard once wrote that the dramatist should not give a plate of food to the audience all cut up and ready to eat; s/he must let the audience cut the food up itself. Similarly, Pinter's essay 'Writing for the Theatre' likens conventional theatre to a crossword puzzle where 'the audience holds the paper. The play fills in the blanks. Everyone's happy.' Reality isn't like this, says Pinter: people, words, and actions are never that straightforward. How can a dramatic character know exactly what he/she wants if real people half the time don't even know their own intentions? This is exactly the problem Michael Frayn poses in his play *Copenhagen* (1998): 'the epistemology of intention'. Pinter's 'mixed feelings about words', what they signify, how ambiguous they can be, expresses a doubt about language that is fundamental to modern drama:

> So often, below the word spoken, is the thing known and unspoken. My characters tell me so much and no more, with reference to their experience, their aspirations, their motives, their history. Between my lack of biographical data about them and the ambiguity of what they say lies a territory which is not only worthy of exploration but which it is compulsory to explore.

Pinter's early plays, which helped establish his unique style of theatre, include *The Birthday Party* (1958), *The Caretaker* (1960), and *The Dumb Waiter* (1960). They helped generate a new word—Pinteresque—meaning a menacing atmosphere in an otherwise ordinary setting, with disturbing silences and unexplained motives. In these early plays, Pinter often has a stranger enter a domestic setting and disrupt it in oblique ways. We don't know why he or she has come; no explanation is given. But the effect is cataclysmic. Families fall apart and rearrange themselves, people die or disappear, all within familiar-looking rooms and relationships and expressed in unremarkable, everyday speech.

And yet these domestic settings are only realistic at first glance; rather like Williams' stage directions in *Cat on a Hot Tin Roof*, which called for deliberately outsized furniture, Pinter in *The Homecoming* (1965) shows us an ordinary living room but with the back wall missing, leaving just a 'square arch shape'. What does this strange arch signify? Is it some kind of symbol—a gaping hole in the family, a Dante-esque entrance to Hell, or a portal to a new life that is about to begin?

Typical of Pinter's style is his crafting of dialogue that seems utterly mundane and harmless but carries some indefinable threat. When Mick in *The Caretaker* tells the homeless intruder about his interior decorating plans, talking of wallpaper and paint, what is he really saying and why does it all seem so menacing? In *The Dumb Waiter*, two hired assassins discuss Eccles cakes, biscuits, and packets of crisps, and bicker about the etymology of the phrase 'put the kettle on' while they await their next assignment, and the mundane content of their talk seems at odds with their job of killing people.

This incongruousness is at the heart of Pinter's drama. The audience senses that what the characters are saying isn't articulating their inner thoughts. Even when a character does say he is speaking sincerely, we can't fully trust him: 'Listen, Sam,' says Max in *The Homecoming*, 'I want to say something to you. From my heart.' Max has assumed the role of mother in his all-male household of brothers and sons, not just wearing an apron and doing housework but even feeling 'the pain of childbirth—I suffered the pain, I've still got the pangs'. While on the surface the play seems profoundly misogynistic, in fact it raises key questions about women's roles, showing how limited they are even while the feminist movement ought to have liberated women; instead their power is still linked to their sexuality, a situation that the Restoration playwright Aphra Behn so well delineated in her play *The Rover* (1677). Hundreds of years later, how much has changed?

When characters in plays do finally drop the verbal bomb of self-revelation, it should be deeply unsettling. But one of Pinter's achievements is to displace the conventional emphasis on revelation of truth and deny such expectations. At the end of the play, Sam suddenly blurts out 'MacGregor had Jessie in the back of my cab as I drove them along', and thereby reveals the family's dark secret, a moment that is so emotionally taxing that he promptly 'croaks and collapses'. Yet this is hardly noticed and it doesn't actually matter; the truth has come too late to affect anything. The past, which has silently shaped and burdened all the characters, suddenly makes no difference in light of the new, equally disturbing future they have just planned in which Ruth will voluntarily be the family whore.

Pinter shares with Williams and Sam Shepard the sense of past sexual events having a defining impact on one's future and one's personality. Shepard's *Buried Child* (1978) pays homage to O'Neill's groundbreaking treatment of dark family secrets (incest and infanticide) in *Desire Under the Elms* and later plays like *Long Day's Journey into Night*, introducing a contemporary element (TV watching as endless, mindless, destructive activity) and a supernatural, mystical event that is never explained: the repeated proliferation of vegetables from barren soil. The image of a mute young man entering with armfuls of carrots that have miraculously grown overnight in his garden makes Shepard one of the most strongly visual playwrights, giving new life to symbolism on stage through a succession of striking theatrical images that also memorably includes a room full of toasters in *True West* (1980).

Pinter, Shepard, Beckett, and Stoppard lead the experimentation with language, minimalism, and structure that characterizes theatre in these decades. The long and spectacular career of Stoppard takes off with *Rosencrantz and Guildenstern are Dead* (1966, Figure 7), set in a kind of Beckettian no-man's-land, offstage from the main action of Shakespeare's *Hamlet*, and it is suffused with existentialist discourse of the kind that, if they could articulate themselves fully, Beckett's characters might just expound. Ros and Guil, symbiotically linked like Didi and Gogo in *Waiting for Godot*, are passing the time; they repeatedly toss coins to test 'the law of probability', 'the law of averages', and 'the law of diminishing returns'. The play's bleak comedy, accentuated

7. **Shades of Beckett: Samuel Barnett and Jamie Parker in a 2011 production of Tom Stoppard's *Rosencrantz and Guildenstern are Dead*, directed by Trevor Nunn, at the Theatre Royal Haymarket, London.**

through its short, sharp exchanges, its storytelling, and its minutely choreographed, repetitive actions, also echoes *Godot*. So does the existential angst: 'We have not been...picked out...simply to be abandoned...set loose to find our own way...We are entitled to some direction...I would have thought.' And, like Beckett's plays, metatheatrical moments break through, as when Guil suddenly looks around 'at the audience' and says: 'You and I, Alfred—we could create a dramatic precedent here.'

The dominant voice in British theatre in these decades, however, is a political one, as the National Theatre is inaugurated in England (1975), and this combined with the Royal Court Theatre puts Britain at the forefront of new writing for the stage. The National Theatre's 1980 production of Howard Brenton's *The Romans in Britain* contained a brief scene of (simulated) anal rape that provoked Mary Whitehouse to bring a private prosecution (though she had not actually seen the play) against the director, Michael Bogdanov, in 1982. This launched, in

Michael Billington's words, 'a new wave of vindictive puritanism'. Yet again, and as it would show many times in subsequent decades, British playwrights were at the forefront of political theatre. Most prominent among these has been Caryl Churchill.

Caryl Churchill and the redefinition of theatre

Because she experiments with many different theatrical styles there is no single definition of a typical Churchill play, just as Gambaro's work defies easy categorization. But as a socialist-feminist playwright Churchill repeatedly stages certain questions, such as what modern feminism means, how capitalism and feminism interact, and how social justice can ever be achieved.

Like many British political playwrights she has been deeply influenced by Brecht, especially in her early work, such as *Light Shining in Buckinghamshire* (1976), *Vinegar Tom* (1976), and *Cloud Nine* (1979). She uses his devices and theories as well as his collaborative working practice, working with theatre companies Joint Stock, Monstrous Regiment, and the Royal Court. Collaboration and improvisation are important to her as a way of resisting replicating the patriarchal mode of the single artistic force dictating the production. She also developed her own trademark overlapping dialogue, now used by many other playwrights from David Mamet to the so-called 'in-yer-face' dramatists of the 1990s.

Top Girls (1982, Figure 8) casts a scathing eye on Thatcher's Britain by exposing a feminism that forces women to gain power by behaving like men—at least, men like the ruthless real estate agents of Mamet's *Glengarry Glen Ross* which premiered at the National Theatre in London in 1983. Like these men, who are so desperate to sell property that any means justify their ends, Marlene has risen to the top of her employment agency by quashing those around her and by sacrificing everything personal—even her daughter Angie, who is being raised by Marlene's sister and thinks Marlene is her aunt.

8. The transhistorical dinner party of famous women that opens Caryl Churchill's *Top Girls*, in a 2008 production at the Biltmore Theatre, Manhattan.

Top Girls begins with a remarkable scene in a restaurant where Marlene is hosting a dinner party to celebrate her promotion, and her guests are a selection of exemplary women from different historical periods and places: Isabella Bird, the Victorian traveller; Lady Nijo, a Japanese geisha; Pope Joan, who disguised herself as a man in order to be pope; Dull Gret, the apron- and armour-clad female fighter in Brueghel's painting 'Dulle Griet'; and Patient Griselda of Chaucer's 'The Clerk's Tale' in *The Canterbury Tales*. As the director Max Stafford-Clark put it, this fantastical opening scene was a forty-minute *coup de théâtre* 'bringing realism to surrealism'.

At first these women do seem extraordinarily successful in their own ways. But they undermine their own achievements by not listening to each other, interrupting and cutting each other's stories off, and tellingly ignoring the lone, silent waitress who serves them. They also constantly refer to the men in their lives. On the page, Churchill's dialogue can be hard to follow (the slashes indicate where the next character is supposed to start speaking):

> ISABELLA: Yes, I forgot all my Latin. But my father was the mainspring of my life and when he died I was so grieved. I'll have the chicken, please,/and the soup.
>
> NIJO: Of course you were grieved. My father was saying his prayers and he dozed off in the sun. So I touched his knee to rouse him. 'I wonder what will happen,' he said, and then he was dead before he finished his sentence./If he'd
>
> MARLENE: What a shock.
>
> NIJO: died saying his prayers he would have gone straight to heaven./Waldorf salad. (Act I)

Later on in the play, Marlene's pronouncement on her hapless adolescent daughter makes an ominous theme: 'She's not going to make it.' She is yet another victim of Marlene's selfishness. Women need to work together, listen to each other, and not replicate competitive strategies if they are to survive and to alter the conditions around them that cause their oppression in the first place. Churchill's method of collaborative creation underscores this point, as does her typical requirement for each actor to play several roles; in *Top Girls*, for example, seven women play sixteen roles in the play. In her play *Cloud Nine* (1979) the role doubling goes even further, as a white woman is played by a man, a black man played by a white man, and a child played by a woman. This is a kind of Brechtian estrangement, destabilizing the link between actor and role as well as questioning essentialist notions of character, gender, sexuality, and race.

Brian Friel and Athol Fugard

Brian Friel, a leading contemporary Irish playwright, began his career at about the same time as Churchill. Friel's plays in this period include *Philadelphia, Here I Come!* (1964), *The Freedom of the City* (1973), *Living Quarters* (1977), *Faith Healer* (1979), *Aristocrats* (1979), and *Translations* (1980). Each of these is remarkable in its own right, and they are totally distinct from one another in dramatic form.

Translations brought movingly to the stage the issue of linguistic imperialism by dramatizing the historical moment when the English army came to Ireland (18th century) to create Ordnance Survey maps—and in order to do this it needed to find English equivalents for difficult local place names. Set in the fictional village of Baile Beag, and showing the repercussions of the army's renaming of cherished local sites and landmarks rich with regional history, the play raises trenchant questions about what gets lost in such a process of translation. The play opens symbolically with the celebration of the christening of a new baby; it closes with that same baby's funeral. In between, tensions mount as local villagers react with hostility to the military cartographers. But language is an organic, living thing and it can 'fossilize', as Hugh, the village teacher, acknowledges. 'Words are signals, counters. They are not immortal. And it can happen... it can happen that a civilization can be imprisoned in a linguistic contour which no longer matches the landscape of... fact.'

The play has a large cast of characters and clearly alludes to contemporary political issues as the Donnelly twins, whom we never see, are at work offstage devising violent acts aimed at undermining the survey mapping and driving out the English. By contrast *Faith Healer* (like Friel's 1993 play *Molly Sweeney*) is a pared down, understated, but no less horrifying drama. It has three actors (two men, one woman) addressing the audience in turn in long monologues. They all tell the same story about Frank, a faith healer, who ends up being killed by a hostile and suspicious audience when he fails to heal a customer. Each teller relates slightly different versions of the same events and people, as each has a different set of motives and memories. Which is the true version? Whom do we trust? It is unsettling to feel drawn to a speaker who is exposing his or her inner self, telling you a compelling story, yet not be sure if you can believe what he or she is saying. As in so many of his plays, Friel challenges the audience's expectations of a play and experiments constantly with dramatic form and staging.

In South Africa, Athol Fugard's theatre has been a vital element in the ongoing struggle against racism and the eventual dismantling of the apartheid regime. Like Friel, Fugard writes political theatre that manages to address current issues while also being lyrical, moving, and enduring. In its very title, *'Master Harold'...and the Boys* (1982) signifies the gulf between Hally, a white teenager, and Sam and Willie, his mother's two black servants. Their relationship seems genuinely warm and the wise 'boys' gently guide and encourage Hally through his various challenges: his history homework, his difficult relationship with his absent father, his loneliness. Fugard movingly employs metaphors to convey the main ideas of the play: a dance competition, symbolizing harmonious encounters between people who navigate carefully around a crowded dance floor without bumping into one another; and a kite Sam once made for Hally to comfort him. But Hally's pressures prove too much for him and the play's simmering racial tension boils over into an ugly confrontation between Sam and Hally that, in a heartbeat, destroys their fragile bond. In the final moments of the play, Sam explains what happened when he made the kite for Hally so long ago but had to leave it tied to a bench:

I couldn't sit down there and stay with you. It was a 'Whites Only' bench. You were too young, too excited to notice then. But not anymore. If you're not careful...Master Harold...you're going to be sitting up there by yourself for a long time to come, and there won't be a kite in the sky.

Theatre and race

Many other playwrights besides Fugard have explored race relations, particularly in America. The growth of the Civil Rights Movement gave rise to a range of plays protesting racism and exploring the African American experience.

Lorraine Hansberry made history as the first black woman to have a play on Broadway: *A Raisin in the Sun* (1959, Figure 9), also the first play on Broadway to be directed by a black director (George C. Wolfe). It was a sensational success, and it emerged from a feeling shared by other minority groups that purportedly 'realistic' plays were not showing everyone's reality. Based on Hansberry's

9. 'A dream deferred': Lorraine Hansberry's *A Raisin in the Sun* featuring Claudia McNeil, Ruby Dee, Sidney Poitier, and Diana Sands in a scene from the 1961 film that was based on the play's Broadway premiere.

own experiences, the play shows a black family in Chicago struggling to move out of poverty and into a white neighbourhood called Clybourne Park. Recently widowed, the family's matriarch, Big Mama, has the insurance money after her husband's death all ready to spend on this big move, but her son Walter, fed up with his job chauffeuring wealthy white people around, persuades her to let him invest most of it in a friend's liquor store. Not only does this friend embezzle the cash but a representative of Clybourne Park comes to offer the family ('you people') money in return for not moving into the development. Big Mama is dismayed when Walter at first seems happy to accept this buy-out. But in the stirring final moments of the play he regains his dignity, asserting that 'we have decided to move into our house because my father—my father—he earned it for us brick by brick.... We don't want your money'.

The subplot of *A Raisin in the Sun*, which furnished material for Hansberry's later, unfinished play *Les Blancs*, shows Walter's twenty-year-old sister Beneatha facing her own challenges: she wants to pursue her dream of getting an education and becoming a doctor, but she is also tempted by the stability offered by suitors George (an assimilated black man) and Asagai, who retains his Nigerian identity and wants her to return to his village with him. In this regard the play explores the problem of 'double consciousness' first articulated by W.E.B. DuBois' *The Souls of Black Folk* (1903). Living with racism takes a constant toll, sabotaging identity and killing aspirations. Walter is, as his mother notices, 'kind of wild in the eyes...always tied up in some kind of knot about something', whereas Asagai knows exactly who he is. Big Mama's misguided, unquestioning conformity to white standards has confused Walter and the play shows him having to find his way back from that upbringing.

Like *Look Back in Anger* a few years before it, *A Raisin in the Sun* was a landmark play for its themes but not for its formal qualities; both plays are fairly conventional, even old-fashioned, in their structure. What was revolutionary about them was what they showed audiences for the first time. Osborne brought a new sense of raw anger to the stage (Jimmy's ranting is similar to Walter Younger's in *Raisin*, though without any of the social injustice Walter has to endure as a black man in America in the 1950s). Hansberry showed Broadway audiences, for the first time, a black family as the focus of the drama (there is only one white character in the play). In a way her play is an answer not so much to Jimmy Porter—surely a rebel without a cause compared to Hansberry's genuinely oppressed Youngers—as to Arthur Miller, Tennessee Williams, Thornton Wilder, and all the other American dramatists whose plays are variations on the theme of the American family but who always show that family to be white (a notable exception is Eugene O'Neill in *All God's Chillun Got Wings*, 1924).

Even though *Raisin* appears to end happily, with the Younger family moving into their new apartment, the audience isn't sure what will happen next: will the family survive in this hostile environment? Will it stay together, given all the internal tensions that threaten it as well as the external ones? While it is on the surface an empowering and uplifting drama, there is a tragic undertone—the racism never goes away, as Bruce Norris suggests in *Clybourne Park* (2010), his sequel to *A Raisin in the Sun*.

Hansberry was daring, but for some she was not daring enough. In *Dutchman* (1964), Amiri Baraka took a less tempered and theatrically more innovative approach to racism. In a New York subway car, a seductive white woman named Lula hits on a studious-looking young black man named Clay (a name suggesting malleable material, too easily moulded). She teases, goads, and insults him, provoking him to a violent explosion of rage against all white people whom, he confesses, he feels he should kill; yet when he backs down, regains his composure, and decides to leave, she stabs him in the heart and orders the other passengers—who have passively looked on throughout the dialogue—to dump his body out of the car at the next stop.

Another young, unsuspecting black man gets in the car, and Lula looks at him: like Ionesco's *The Lesson* (1951), the play ends with the suggestion that this is her next victim, that this ritual killing will be repeated endlessly. The last thing the audience sees is an old black conductor doing a soft shoe shuffle and tipping his hat to Lula.

One of the plays Hansberry left behind at her tragic death from cancer at age thirty-four, and which was completed by her husband, attests to her continuing search for ways to fight racism through the theatre. She began working on *Les Blancs* (*The Whites*) after seeing French playwright Jean Genet's *Les Negres* (*The Blacks*, 1959) which she felt evaded the issue of colonial oppression in Africa by romanticizing and exoticizing Africans. She also felt that Genet's absurdism obscured the real and urgent issues in his drama. At the start of his play, Genet explains in a note that the play is 'intended for a white audience', but if it is ever performed before a black audience, 'then a white person, male or female, should be invited every evening', welcomed formally by the director and seated in the front row centre, with the 'spotlight...focused upon this symbolic white throughout the performance'. If no white person agreed to do that, 'then let white masks be distributed to the black spectators as they enter the theatre'. Hansberry rejects such coyness; *Les Blancs* opens with a tableau and soundscape powerfully evoking the African bush and showing a majestic black woman warrior triumphantly pulling an enormous spear from the earth and brandishing it above her head.

These plays confront the issues of postcolonial cultures and throw the American Civil Rights struggle into wider relief. They depict American situations and characters, but often transplant them into indigenous African settings, or at least evoke them. *Les Blancs* depicts the struggle between natives and colonizers in an African village. Similarly, Nigerian playwright Wole Soyinka, the first African writer to win the Nobel Prize in Literature (1986), dramatized the tensions within tribal culture in Africa in plays like *Death and the King's*

Horseman (1976), showing the violence done to native culture in a Yoruba village. In a move made by many postcolonial playwrights, Soyinka also adapted existing plays to reflect contemporary African politics and issues of race, notably *Opera Wonyosi* (1977), his reworking of Brecht and Weill's *Threepenny Opera*. Similarly, Aimé Césaire (from Martinique) in his version of *The Tempest*, called *Une Tempête* (1969), reimagined Shakespeare's *The Tempest* focusing on Caliban as postcolonial subject.

Experimental performance

In these decades a strong strain of experimental, avant-garde theatre springs up across Europe and America that thoroughly dismantles concepts and entities like 'the audience' or 'the actor' or 'the play'. Peter Weiss's *Marat/Sade* (1964) attempts to stage some of Artaud's ideas about the theatre of cruelty as well as drawing on Brechtian techniques. Jerzy Grotowski's Polish Laboratory Theatre, established in 1959 and one of the most influential experimental theatre companies of the late 20th century, also grew directly out of the ideas of Artaud. He mounted a range of productions that toured globally and aimed at 'a direct, unmediated contact between actors and spectators, a "total act" that required an ascetic physical and spiritual discipline from the performers', as theatre historian W.B. Worthen puts it.

Grotowski's Poor Theatre stripped theatre down to its core—the relationship between actor and audience—to explore what Grotowski called the 'perceptual, direct, live communion' that issued from it. In one compelling example of his practice, Grotowski asked his company to go off and build a house that would become the set of a play. When they had finished the job, they came and said they were ready for the performance now that the house was done. He said that they were already finished: building the house *was* the performance.

Chapter 6
Bearing witness: drama since 1980

Theatre doesn't just show us a problem or capture the essence of a particular time and place, it can also effect change. This is particularly striking in contemporary theatre which is so rich in playwrights who in their long careers have devoted themselves to bringing about political and social change. As John McGrath wrote, 'It is a public event, and it is about matters of public concern.... The theatre is by its nature a political forum.'

Athol Fugard's outspokenly critical plays against apartheid in South Africa helped to bring it to the scrutiny of the outside world. The late Václav Havel, once imprisoned for his absurdist political dramas, eventually became president of the new Czech Republic. For decades Brian Friel's powerful dramas have helped shape public understanding of the 'Troubles' in Ireland. Edward Albee continues to produce thought-provoking, original plays tackling social hypocrisy and prejudice, both in America and beyond. This list goes on: Harold Pinter (who died in 2008 and who won the Nobel Prize in Literature), Caryl Churchill, Adrienne Kennedy, Sam Shepard, David Mamet, and many others.

However, these playwrights also all *transcend* the boundaries of their own time; their themes go beyond the topical, so that their plays endure as drama long after the particular issue they treat has been addressed. As the late British playwright Pam Gems put it, 'all theatre is political in a profound way. It can, without resort to the vote or the gun, alter climate, change opinion, laugh prejudice out the door, soften hearts, awaken perception.'

A good deal of this chapter is devoted to British playwrights because many of the leading plays and developments in recent drama have come from Britain. This goes a long way back. As we saw earlier with Oscar Wilde and Bernard Shaw, British playwrights have long considered themselves to be the conscience (or the gadfly) of their age, and used all kinds of inventive ways to get around theatre censorship while tackling sensitive issues. This political engagement only intensified over the course of the 20th century, for instance in the thorough embrace of Brecht's ideas after 1956. A fiercely critical left-wing theatre tradition emerged, finding a home in the National Theatre and at the Royal Court, and the Thatcher years pushed politics even more firmly centre stage as playwrights from Churchill and Bond to Brenton and Hare deeply criticized what they saw as the government's relentless erosion of the post-war social and political framework that had made Britain a humane place to live—universal health care and free university education, housing and welfare benefits, state pensions.

These topics also came with startlingly fresh and original theatrical innovations that made theatre itself new, even while it tackled specific problems and broke seemingly age-old taboos. Theatre since 1980 is marked by a number of striking new forms, movements, and innovations, ushered in by a plethora of fresh new playwrights bursting on the scene as well as the ongoing work of long-established playwrights. Through developments like verbatim theatre—a renewal of documentary drama—and 'in-yer-face' theatre, drama in recent decades has been breaking taboos and fundamentally challenging what is acceptable for theatrical representation.

1995 and all that

Sarah Kane's *Blasted* (1995) shattered previous paradigms of stage violence and redrew the lines of what could be shown in a theatre. Critics for the most part recoiled in horror at a play that featured rape, torture, and cannibalism taking place in a hotel room in Leeds. The response echoed the reaction to Ibsen's *Ghosts* (a play that includes a character with syphilis) at its London premiere in 1891—'a loathsome sore unbandaged...an open drain'—and some critics dismissed *Blasted*'s violence as cheap and gratuitous: 'a sustained onslaught on the sensibilities...Sheer, unadulterated brutalism' wrote the *Evening Standard*; 'this disgusting feast of filth' wrote the *Daily Mail*.

It is true that *Blasted* contains stage directions like 'the Soldier puts his mouth over one of Ian's eyes, sucks it out, bites it off and eats it' and 'he eats the [dead] baby'. But such shocking acts are not unimaginable, especially in a war zone: Kane was making a connection with real-world events in the Balkans, a drama of horrific violence, ethnic cleansing, mass rape, and killing shown on TV news for years. Like Bond's *Saved* decades earlier, *Blasted* asks deeply uncomfortable questions about how violence can become ordinary and 'normalized' and why we ignore horror and atrocity right on our doorsteps.

'In-yer-face' theatre

Blasted helped to usher in a new era of more violent, overtly sexual drama exemplified by the work of playwrights such as Mark Ravenhill, Martin McDonagh, Jez Butterworth, Patrick Marber, Tracy Letts, David Greig, David Harrower, Anthony Neilson, Joe Penhall, Philip Ridley, Conor McPherson, Martin Crimp, Simon Stephens, and Sebastian Barry.

Ravenhill's *Shopping and Fucking* (1996) solidified the link that Joe Orton had made so explicit between sex and violence, and placed it within the context of a contemporary culture of unbridled consumerism. Sex, drugs, theft—all these are mere commodities, and relationships just another set of transactions in a culture emblematized by the Harvey Nichols department store and the giant shopping mall. Like Patrick Marber's *Closer* (1997), sex is at a remove: once the most intimate experience, phone sex and Internet sex make it the most impersonal and interchangeable. Casual sex supplants meaningful intimacy.

Closer also revolves around deceit, betrayal, and lying—the same themes that are central to Hellman's *The Children's Hour* and Williams' *Cat on a Hot Tin Roof*, as discussed earlier, but where Williams hammers the theme home in rather didactic terms, *Closer* alludes to it more through the actions than the words of the characters.

Lying is also at the heart of Martin McDonagh's hyper-violent play *The Lieutenant of Inishmore* (2001), in which a lie told by a character in order to preserve his life sets in motion a series of increasingly violent events completely out of proportion to the deed being covered up. Davey has accidentally killed his neighbour's cat, Wee Thomas. But this is no ordinary neighbour: Padraic is a pathologically violent, unhinged ex-IRA guerrilla (kicked out of the IRA for 'being too mad'), and Wee Thomas has been his sole friend for fifteen years. Terrified of Padraic's vengeful wrath, Davey attempts to hide the truth through a hilarious, blackly comic set of actions, including stealing another cat and painting it black with shoe polish to pass it off as Wee Thomas. Everything goes wrong, and by the end of the play the stage is littered with blood and body parts. Stunned, the audience suddenly hears meowing and sees a black cat saunter nonchalantly on to this scene of senseless devastation; it is Wee Thomas, alive and well. It turns out it was another cat that had been killed, so all of this violence was for nothing. But is violence ever 'for' something? The play puts this troubling question to the audience and makes it face its own pleasure in McDonagh's disturbingly comic 'take' on murder, sadism, torture, and revenge.

Sex and sensibility

In an interview in 1984, Churchill noted that American drama tended to be more psychological and more focused on individual, personal experience and the family, an approach quite different from her (and other British dramatists') way of looking at 'the larger context of groups of people...at bigger things'. Martin Esslin put it more bluntly in 1988, saying that American drama was too narrowly focused on dysfunctional families and their quarrelling parents and children, resulting in what Benedict Nightingale called 'diaper drama' compared to the British theatre's powerful engagement with contemporary political issues.

All of that changed with *Angels in America* (1991), a two-part epic (both in the generic and the Brechtian sense) that caused protests across America for its frank depiction of homosexuality and AIDS, including simulated gay sex (though it is only figurative, as the partners are standing on opposite sides of the stage). The play, whose two parts are *Millennium Approaches* and *Perestroika*, interweaves several seemingly unrelated stories, showing their surprising connections in the end through the characters' redrawn relationships.

Troubling, sad, funny, and sharp, *Angels* dismantles stubbornly entrenched myths about the founding values of America, its claim to be a harmonious melting-pot of cultures, and its pressures to conform to norms of religion, marriage, family, sexuality, and gender. It depicts real historical characters, like the vicious lawyer Roy Cohn and his most famous victim, Ethel Rosenberg, convicted of being a communist spy and executed for treason, and blends them with fictional ones like Harper Pitt, the wife of promising young law clerk Joe who, like Roy Cohn, refuses to admit that he is homosexual and keeps up a pretence of 'normal' married life. Joe and Harper's Mormonism puts additional pressures on them to enact typical heterosexual behaviour but everything falls apart as Harper becomes increasingly dependent on Valium to escape her problems. The hallucinations she experiences as a result give the play some of its most hilarious and extraordinarily inventive, powerful scenes, especially one in a history museum in which a life-size diorama of the Mormons on their westward march suddenly comes alive and the characters start talking to Harper.

There were many important gay plays and plays about AIDS before *Angels in America*, such as Mart Crowley's *The Boys in the Band* (1968), Martin Sherman's *Bent* (1979), Harvey Fierstein's *Torch Song Trilogy* (1982), and Larry Kramer's *The Normal Heart* (1985), as well as new theatre companies like the lesbian-feminist performance troupe Split Britches (since 1980), all of which broke new ground, bringing sexuality and politics directly into the theatre and challenging the dominant realistic mode of performance and structure.

But *Angels* was on a larger scale in every sense. The most striking instance of this is the huge angel that appears in a hallucination before Prior, the AIDS-stricken character at the centre of the play who sees this vision hovering above his hospital bed (Figure 10). Kushner's stage directions indicate that the angel should not look too other-worldly; the audience should see the rigging, the cage in which the actor hangs, and the occasional feathers coming off. In this and other aspects, such as the epic span of the play, *Angels* is firmly in the tradition of Brecht, exposing the illusion and artifice of theatre.

Edward Albee in his play *The Goat; or, Who is Sylvia?* (2002) broke one further, and perhaps final, taboo, that of interspecies sex. Highly successful, prize-winning architect Martin has fallen in love with Sylvia—a goat with lovely brown eyes. He confides in his best

10. No ordinary hospital visit: a hallucination scene from Tony Kushner's *Angels in America*, in a 2010 production by Signature Theatre Company, New York.

friend, who—like the idealistic Gregers Werle in Ibsen's *The Wild Duck*—high-mindedly takes it upon himself to inform Martin's wife Stevie about this unusual extramarital affair. Utter devastation ensues as Stevie and their teenage son's world falls apart.

Albee said that his aim as a playwright was to make 'people imagine what they cannot conceive of imagining, to imagine how they would feel if they were in this situation, to learn something about the nature of love, of tolerance, and consciousness'. The play, mixing the comic and the tragic, attains something akin to the status of Greek tragedy as Stevie's rage culminates in her Clytemnestra-like killing of Sylvia, bringing the carcass on stage and dumping it there in full view of the audience as the play ends.

Identity politics

Both Kushner and Albee address head-on the price paid for concealing or repressing one's true self and identity in order to conform to societal expectations. This is also a dominant concern of African American dramatists.

Among the standout dramas in August Wilson's ten-play cycle, each play representing a decade in the 20th-century black American experience, are *Fences* (1985) and *Ma Rainey's Black Bottom* (1982). In the latter play, set in Chicago in the 1920s (the jazz age), a group of famous black blues musicians records their music in a studio managed by white producers. The tensions among the musicians are more intense and destructive than those between the group and the producers, erupting into violence and murder and showing the devastating consequences of an internalized racism. 'You just a leftover from history', says Toledo, the trumpeter, to a fellow musician. In the contemporary stew of life, a mixture of all different races and peoples,

> the colored man is the leftovers. Now, what's the colored man gonna do with himself? That's what we waiting to find out.... We don't know that we been took [by the white man] and made history out of. Done went and filled the white man's belly and now he's full and tired and wants you to get out of the way and let him be by himself.

In satirical and comic mode, George C. Wolfe's *The Colored Museum* (1986) uncomfortably suggests that it is internalized acquiescence in black stereotypes as much as society's racism that limits African Americans. This had been Luis Valdez's strategy in his short play *Los Vendidos* (*The Sellouts*, 1967), performed by his Teatro Campesino, which brilliantly presents a succession of Chicano stereotypes in order to undermine them. The eleven 'exhibits' or sketches that make up *The Colored Museum* include 'Cooking with Aunt Ethel' and 'The Last Mama-on-the-Couch', parodies of the overbearing black matriarch well known from Hansberry's *A Raisin in the Sun*, whose Broadway production Wolfe had directed. In very different styles, these diverse plays are asking: what *is* black identity?

A further important dramatization of this question occurs in Anna Deavere Smith's *Fires in the Mirror* (1992) and *Twilight: Los Angeles* (1994), which are verbatim dramas with a twist: she not only wrote them but performed all the roles. Smith was troubled by the violent riots brought about by the Rodney King beatings in Los Angeles and the Crown Heights killings of a black boy and a young Jewish man who were innocent victims of simmering ethnic, racial, and religious hatred. Embarking on a search for no less than 'American identity', she interviewed dozens of participants in these two major events in modern American history and transcribed selections of the interviews word for word—including hesitations, ums and ahs, incoherent sentences, and half-finished thoughts—arranged like poetry on the page. She then toured the country with the one-woman show in which she moves seamlessly in and out of each character, whether black or white, Jewish or non-Jewish, male or female, using just a few props to change characters, all evoked by Smith using their own words in order to give a balanced and provocative view of contemporary social problems. This format raises vital questions about the viability of the form itself, whether it is reliant on her as performer or whether it lends itself to other interpreters.

Many other playwrights are exploring and exposing the racial fault lines running through contemporary cultures. Ayub Khan-Din's *East is East* (1999) and Kwame Kwei-Armah's *Elmina's Kitchen* (2003) address, in very different ways, the strains and pressures of double consciousness raised much earlier by Lorraine Hansberry and Amiri Baraka, particularly the generational rift as parents and children see cultural assimilation differently. This dilemma is likewise dramatized through Timberlake Wertenbaker's play *After Darwin* (1998), at whose centre is the haunting story of Jemmy Button, taken from his native Tierra del Fuego by Captain FitzRoy during his and Darwin's voyage on the *Beagle*, acclimatized to English culture, and then brought back to live—unhappily—among his original tribe. This experiment in biculturalism did not work; Jemmy died poor and alone, not fitting into either environment, and Wertenbaker situates this historical moment within contemporary experience.

After Darwin, like Wertenbaker's hugely successful stage adaptation of Thomas Keneally's novel *Our Country's Good* (1988), is an example of historiographic metatheatre: plays in which, as theatre scholar Alexander Feldman notes, 'self-reflexive engagements with the traditions and forms of dramatic art illuminate historical themes and aid in the representation of historical events'. In other words, playwrights nestle a bit of real history (Darwin and FitzRoy on the *Beagle*, the founding of Australia in 1788 with English convicts and their encounter with indigenous peoples, while also putting on a play) within a made-up framework, or vice versa, in order to foreground the unreliability of received historical narratives.

Renewing documentary theatre

This questioning of reliability is part of a broader current within contemporary drama to distrust history and its makers. Like Brian Friel before him (*Making History*, 1989), Alan Bennett is a playwright interested in the vexed question of what 'history' is—certainly not, for these playwrights, a neutral, objective thing, but one full of bias, distortion, even outright lies. A good example is Bennett's *The History Boys* (2004), which shows a group of students in a private school in England preparing for their final exams and getting ready for university while dealing with a brash new history teacher, Mr Irwin, who proclaims: 'History nowadays is not a matter of conviction. It's a performance. It's entertainment. And if it isn't, make it so.'

Yet at the same time, there has been a wave of plays, dubbed 'verbatim theatre', that goes in the opposite direction, their dialogue constructed solely out of actual words spoken by real people, not 'made up'. Among these are Richard Norton-Taylor's *The Colour of Justice* (1999), Lucy Prebble's *Enron* (2009), David

Hare's *Stuff Happens* (2004), and Moises Kaufman's *The Laramie Project* (2000), each depicting a moment of crisis, crime, and injustice whose repercussions are still being profoundly felt.

The Colour of Justice re-enacts verbatim the trials of the white youths accused of stabbing to death black teenager Stephen Lawrence in London and the police mishandling of the case. *The Laramie Project* explores another hate crime, the 1998 murder of homosexual student Matthew Shepard in Wyoming by two young men who are now serving life sentences for the killing. Drawing on over 200 interviews with Laramie's citizens, Kaufman and colleagues at Tectonic Theater Company constructed a play that explores the repercussions of the killing on the town using only eight actors who play more than sixty characters. The focus is not so much on justice, which was done in this case, but the aftermath of such a crime within its community as well as the wider world, and the need for better legislation to prevent it.

The other two verbatim plays mentioned in this list take a look not at individual crimes but group corruption. *Stuff Happens* examines the words and actions of those involved in the events that led to the Iraq War starting in 2003: primarily Tony Blair, George Bush, Colin Powell, Condoleezza Rice, and Donald Rumsfeld, whose throwaway comment in response to events in Iraq gives the play its title: 'Stuff happens...and it's untidy and freedom's untidy'. *Enron* likewise uses actual dialogue spoken by the real people involved in the corruption that led to America's biggest corporate scandal in recent years, resulting in devastating financial losses to millions of ordinary citizens.

Like Churchill's *Serious Money* (1987), *Enron* takes a hard look at financial greed and corruption, only Prebble depicts actual events as they unfolded. The play also introduces music, singing, dancing, and even fantasy in the form of life-size raptors that prowl around the CEO's office and symbolize his greed and deception. *Enron* is full of whimsical fun like this, including a *Star*

Wars-like lightsaber dance when California's electricity is deregulated allowing the company to raise its prices. Like her predecessor Hallie Flanagan Davis in *e=mc²* (1948), one of the last of the Living Newspapers that I discussed earlier, which gave a thoughtful and entertaining look at the pros and cons of nuclear energy, Prebble shows that verbatim theatre is a flexible form that can integrate the authentic with the creative.

Indeed, verbatim theatre has its roots in such earlier documentary dramas, including *Inherit the Wind* by Lawrence and Lee (1955) and Heinar Kipphardt's *In the Matter of J. Robert Oppenheimer* (1964). The difference now revolves around the issue of authenticity. These earlier examples all laid bare the inherent artifice in the scripts, explaining in their prefaces that while every effort has been made to draw only on the actual words spoken, some measure of imagination and creativity has necessarily entered in through the arrangement and structure of the plays. In other words, their representation of the truth is not word for word. In contemporary verbatim theatre, a greater claim to authenticity is often at stake, which has raised some criticisms from playwrights like David Edgar who object to the assumption that greater truth resides in plays crafted from real words than in fictional drama with its made-up characters and dialogue. Why should *The Laramie Project* be more authentic than *Arcadia* or *Top Girls*? (See Box 3.)

Box 3 What is Art?

While all of these plays were dismantling the concept of truth and history, another hit drama of this period, Yasmina Reza's play *Art* (1996), was pulling apart another big idea. This French play, an international success and still widely performed, asked a pressing question that hasn't been answered yet and may never be: what *is* art? It also asks a much more disturbing question, tied directly to this: what is *friendship*?

Box 3 Continued

Serge has bought an expensive painting that is apparently a blank canvas: the audience doesn't see it until the end so we can't judge for ourselves, which is the clever crux of the play—we listen to Serge arguing with his friends about whether the painting was worth the money, whether it is a piece or art or worthless rubbish as his friend Marc believes, but we have no way of judging it ourselves. A third friend, Yves, tries to straddle these two views but does more harm than good. The friendships fall apart because the questions about art get at larger questions about genuineness and sincerity: 'how much truth and honesty human beings can stand', as Michael Billington puts it.

This book is by no means a tale of two cities (New York and London). Playwrights around the world have been experimenting with new forms and adapting old ones. Lars Norén in Sweden has probed in darkly comic manner the ways in which relationships twist and mutate when they become 'brutal struggles to escape' (Harry Lane). Often his plays, written mostly in the 1980s, centre around a family gathering and the tensions that erupt from long-suppressed desires and hostilities. There is more than a hint of O'Neill and Chekhov in such dramas of tortured family relationships.

Finnish playwrights Sofi Oksanen's and Laura Ruohonen's plays range widely in terms of themes and forms. Oksanen made her debut with *Purge* (*Puhdistus*, 2007), which had its American premiere at La MaMa Experimental Theatre Club in 2011, powerfully interweaving history with sexual and political violence. Ruohonen's *Olga* (1995) portrays a *Harold and Maude*-like relationship between an old woman and young man bringing two marginalized people together, while *Sotaturistit* (*War Tourists*, 2008) reveals, with a disturbingly comic touch, the irresistibility of war.

Israeli playwright Joshua Sobol's many plays are widely known in Europe, and they serve as an antidote to the American drama's tendency to focus too narrowly on the family, as both Nightingale and Esslin criticized. For example, each of the three plays in *Ghetto Triptych* takes place in a different public space, such as a theatre or a hospital. 'I have entire communities as the protagonists of my plays rather than individuals', he has said. 'We are not following the private stories into private locations. If we get a glimpse of private stories, we get that glimpse; we only get edges and scraps that we could observe in that setting.' They also show theatre as essential to human life, just as Wertenbaker does in her stage adaptation of Thomas Keneally's *Our Country's Good* (1988).

Science on stage

Modern drama has always engaged with science—Brecht's *Life of Galileo* stands as a key example—but more and more plays dealing with scientific themes and figures have emerged since the 1980s. There are a number of possible reasons for this. Science has become more accessible, for example through the Internet, and its discoveries get disseminated more quickly and more widely than ever before. At the same time, the more science can do, and the more it tells us about the human body and the natural world, the more responsibility it gives us for its uses—whether the issue is nuclear energy, genetic manipulation, or climate change.

Michael Frayn's *Copenhagen* (1998) and Tom Stoppard's *Hapgood* (1988) both explore, in very different ways, Heisenberg's uncertainty principle, Frayn scrutinizing the inscrutability of human intention (did Heisenberg deliberately withhold his knowledge of how to use physics to construct atomic bombs so that Hitler could not win the war? Or did he really not know how to do the necessary calculations? We are never sure, and neither is he) and Stoppard cleverly using 'uncertainty' as a metaphor for espionage.

Science plays take all manner of forms. Stoppard's *Arcadia* (1993) blends science (mathematics and chaos theory) with an array of other disciplines including art history, literature, and landscape gardening, and uses the stage to integrate them through the device of a simple prop: a large table that remains centre stage throughout the play and accumulates objects common to both time periods in which the play is set (1809 and modern day). The divide between 'the two cultures' is shown to be pointless; 'it's wanting to know that makes us matter' and brings everyone together in common pursuit of knowledge. Much more briefly and starkly, Caryl Churchill's *A Number* (2002) deals with genetics and cloning as an ageing father meets the many sons he had cloned decades ago from his first son, whom he had mistreated and regards as a failed experiment, the cloning being an attempt to correct that mistake and expiate his guilt. The play argues that nurture, not nature, determines who we are.

Contemporary science plays have increasingly explored the mysterious and disturbing terrain of the human psyche and its seemingly innumerable neurological conditions. Joe Penhall's intense three-hander *Blue/Orange* (2000) broke new ground in depicting schizophrenia, 'one of the last great taboos' as the senior doctor in the play puts it. By making the patient black and his doctors white, Penhall raises important issues about racial prejudice and mental health treatment. Lucy Prebble's *The Effect* (2012) dramatizes the hidden world of drug trials and their impact on individual participants, imagining a man and woman involved in trials of a new antidepressant falling in love yet torn apart by the increasingly distressing symptoms he experiences, something that Sarah Kane explored earlier in her disturbing and fragmentary autobiographical play, *4:48 Psychosis* (2000). Most recently, Stoppard's *The Hard Problem* (2015) explores the so-called 'last frontier' of science—what is human consciousness?—with the textual density and pace of a TED talk.

Postmodern theatre

It may well be that science has gained a footing on stage partly because of scientists: 'science plays' often focus on strong characters fighting for their ideas, whether real-life scientists like Niels Bohr, Werner Heisenberg, and Rosalind Franklin or made-up ones. Audiences often seem to crave such definite, even controversial, figures, while in fact the very notion of character is constantly being questioned by contemporary playwrights.

Alan Ayckbourn's *Woman in Mind* (1985), for instance, shows the turmoil and instability of an ordinary, suburban woman gradually losing her grip, having hallucinations, fragmenting before our eyes, as Harper Pitt does in *Angels in America*. Anthony Neilson's *The Wonderful World of Dissocia* (2002) likewise focuses on the female experience of mental illness and hallucination. All of these plays suggest an inherent instability and fractured quality to human identity: not to be dismissed as a disorder affecting only the few any more, but—as mental health campaigners famously put it—'one in four' of us.

This fragmentation of identity is consistent with what Elinor Fuchs in *The Death of Character* calls 'a dispersed idea of self' that is typical of postmodernism and is represented in many different ways in contemporary theatre. But it goes way back. Already Pirandello in the 1920s destabilized the notion of a fixed character. Beckett repeatedly explored the self and its essence, what is merely accidental and what is fundamental; think of Mouth in *Not I* refusing coherent selfhood or Krapp mulling over his past selves preserved on tape. Which one is the truest self?

These ideas are also consistent with what Hans-Thies Lehmann calls 'postdramatic theatre' (explained concisely by Marvin Carlson in *Theatre: A Very Short Introduction*), which shifts the emphasis away from the drama itself (story, character, themes) and on to the material conditions of performance. The postdramatic theatre movement has had a profound impact on playwriting and directing since the late 1990s, especially in Germany led by Heiner Müller in Berlin. Other leading practitioners include Robert Wilson and The Wooster Group, both based in New York, and Forced Entertainment in the UK.

But it is difficult to defamiliarize the notion of character altogether. Though it may be highly elusive or abstract—for example in the austere, seemingly plotless, neo-Beckettian plays of Norwegian playwright Jon Fosse—as long as there is an actor on stage, the idea of character will be present, because there will always be implicit through the human body some basic interaction with social reality.

Adaptations

Modern drama is both groundbreaking and nostalgic for its own origins, a 'haunted stage' as Marvin Carlson puts it. As this book has shown, new plays are constantly being written, but there is also a strong tradition of reinvention.

Some of the most iconic modern dramas get revisited and reimagined in fresh ways, seen through a contemporary lens that shows us something new in them but also recaptures what made them so pioneering in the first place. Simon Stephens' adaptation of Ibsen's *A Doll's House*, for instance, makes the language very current while retaining the relevance of the gender struggle. Sam Adamson has adapted several of Ibsen's plays so loosely as to give them new titles, for instance *Mrs Affleck* (2009), an adaptation of *Little Eyolf*. Pam Gems, Brian Friel, and Michael Frayn have all translated Chekhov, and Friel has infused Chekhov into his own plays like *Performance* and *The Home Place* in setting, themes, and tone. Even so recent a playwright as Samuel Beckett has inspired many subsequent playwrights, including Stoppard, Pinter, Frayn, and Fosse ('Europe's Most Performed Writer' according to *The*

Independent), who takes Beckettian minimalism to an even further extreme in plays like *I Am the Wind* (translated by Stephens), performed at the Young Vic in London in 2011.

This trend is quite apart from the popular current of contemporary theatre that revisits even older drama, the classics of Greek theatre, Golden Age Spanish and Italian drama, Molière, Shakespeare, the Jacobeans. Many modern playwrights have devoted themselves to this kind of renewal; Heiner Müller, for example, followed Brecht's view of using pre-existing material and adapting it to his own purposes, much as Shakespeare had done in his time. Notable modern versions of Greek drama include Marina Carr's *By the Bog of the Cats*, which sets Euripides' *Medea* in contemporary Ireland; Charles L. Mee's *Big Love*, an adaptation of Aeschylus' *The Suppliants*; and the Nobel Prize-winning Austrian playwright and novelist Elfriede Jelinek's plays about the Iraq War based on Aeschylus' *The Oresteia*.

Coda

No book on modern drama would be complete without at least acknowledging the impact of cinema, as noted already in earlier chapters, even if it's not possible to do justice to this topic. Cinema already posed a threat to theatre from its inception (though there has also been much mutual give and take between these two art forms), and Mary Ann Witt has argued that it—along with 'all the new media'—is even more of a threat to postmodern and contemporary theatre, pushing theatre into 'a defensive position'. Director Ian Rickson simply says that theatre has to do what cinema cannot.

Rickson is part of another development that has had an immeasurable impact on modern drama: the rise of the director. Since the late 19th century, when the director was born out of the old actor-manager, the modern theatre has been increasingly defined by directors working collaboratively to devise new

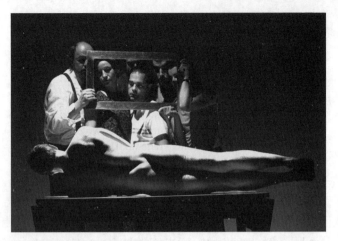

11. Two stories converge on a table, intermingling past and present, as Virgil becomes the Iceman in Simon McBurney/Complicite's devised play *Mnemonic* (1999).

theatrical material or to reshape already existing plays. This has been an exciting worldwide development. All along I have been mentioning some of the key directors of the modern theatre; very recent examples include Alvis Hermanis with the New Riga Theatre in Latvia, a leading exponent of postdramatic theatre, Theatre NO99 in Estonia led by Tiit Ojasoo and Ene-Liis Semper, and Katie Mitchell and Simon McBurney in the UK (see Figure 11).

Complicite, McBurney's company of actors from many different countries and backgrounds, also continues the kind of intercultural theatre pioneered by directors Eugenio Barba, Peter Brook, and Ariane Mnouchkine. When Mnouchkine founded her Théâtre du Soleil in 1964 she, like Brook, sought to bring together various influences from Artaud (expanding the expressive means of performance) to Brecht (raising social awareness) to Copeau, Vilar, and others to establish a people's theatre founded on the act of collective creation. Notably she collaborated with French feminist theorist Hélène Cixous in the 1980s on two epic plays about Cambodia and India.

This intercultural interest is shared by Brook, who with Micheline Rozan established the International Centre of Theatre Research in 1970 in an abandoned music hall in Paris, assembling a company of actors, acrobats, dancers, and mimes from all over the world to create collaborative theatre that would transcend national boundaries. One of its crowning productions was the nine-hour version of the foundational Indian religious epic *The Mahabharata* in 1985, which took place in a quarry near Avignon, France. These productions are founded on deep, on-site cultural and theatrical research of the kind Eugenio Barba's Odin Teatret in Denmark exemplifies; inspired by his studies with Grotowski, Barba pioneered a widely influential acting and directing approach that he calls 'theatre anthropology'. Common to all these enterprises is the ideal of the collective, group approach to devising a new work of theatre and an organic basis in cultural practices experienced first-hand by the company's members.

One of the most hotly debated subjects within modern drama is the degree to which it is the playwright or the director who is dominant. Marvin Carlson asserts that the rise of the director in the late 19th century was the most radical change to happen to theatre in modern times, so much so that 'the dominant figure in the modern European theatre is no longer the actor or the playwright but the director'. Michael Billington argues exactly the opposite, passionately insisting on the primacy of the playwright even while acknowledging the powerful contributions of directors: 'The dramatist is the key creative figure in theatre.... The interpretive arts of acting and directing depend upon the existence of an author's words'.

An introduction to modern drama will tend to endorse the latter view, since it trots out one great play after another. But the fact is that many of these works were brought to life through directors and designers—Jo Mielziner's productions of Miller and Williams, for instance, or Jose Quintero's O'Neill productions of the 1950s—and indeed many of the playwrights who shaped modern drama were also (and sometimes first and foremost) directors and theorists: Gordon Craig, Brecht, Artaud. Finally, some playwrights, like Joan Littlewood with her Theatre Workshop and Caryl Churchill with Monstrous Regiment, prefer a workshopping process that involves the creative team in the development of the play, rather than writing a finished work for the team to perform. The line between playwright and director is often blurred, as in the transcultural devised theatre of Peter Brook, Eugenio Barba, and Simon McBurney.

Whether it is the playwright or the director who provides the source of the theatrical event, the final outcome—what the audience experiences—is paramount. Sarah Kane once said that she went to the theatre 'in the hope that someone in a darkened room somewhere will show me an image that burns itself into my mind'. The plays in this book, as well as the hundreds that had to be left out, all testify to this unique power of modern drama to burn brightly and to smoulder in the mind long after the performance itself is just a memory.

Further reading

The following list provides a sampling of the leading texts on various aspects of modern drama and theatre in English and also serves as an acknowledgement of some of the main sources used in this book.

Ackerman, Alan and Martin Puchner, eds, *Against Theatre: Creative Destructions on the Modernist Stage*, London: Palgrave Macmillan, 2006.

Artaud, Antonin, *The Theatre and its Double*, trans. M.C. Richard, New York: Grove Press, 1958.

Banham, Martin, ed., *The Cambridge Guide to Theatre*, New York: Cambridge University Press, 1995.

Benedict Nightingale, *There Really is a World Beyond 'Diaper Drama'*, New York Times (1 January 1984).

Bennett, Michael Y., *Reassessing the Theatre of the Absurd: Camus, Beckett, Ionesco, Genet, and Pinter*, London: Palgrave Macmillan, 2011.

Bhatia, Nandi, *Modern Indian Theatre: A Reader*, Oxford: Oxford University Press, 2009.

Bigsby, C.W.E., *A Critical Introduction to Twentieth-Century American Drama, vol. 1: 1900–1940*, Cambridge: Cambridge University Press, 1982.

Bigsby, C.W.E., *Modern American Drama, 1945–1990*, Cambridge: Cambridge University Press, 1992.

Billington, Michael, *State of the Nation: British Theatre since 1945*, London: Faber and Faber, 2007.

Billington, Michael, *The 101 Greatest Plays: From Antiquity to the Present*, London: Faber and Faber, 2015.

Blackadder, Neil, *Performing Opposition: Modern Theater and the Scandalized Audience*, Westport, CT: Praeger, 2003.

Brecht, Bertolt, *Brecht on Theatre*, ed. Marc Silberman, Steve Giles, and Tom Kuhn, 3rd edition, London: Bloomsbury, 2015.

Brockett, Oscar, and Robert Findlay, *Century of Innovation: A History of European and American Theatre and Drama since the Late Nineteenth Century*, 2nd edition, Boston: Allyn and Bacon, 1991.

Brook, Peter, *The Empty Space: A Book about the Theatre*, New York: Touchstone, 1968.

Carlson, Marvin, *Theatre: A Very Short Introduction*, Oxford: Oxford University Press, 2014.

Carney, Sean, 'New English Tragedians', in *The Politics and Poetics of Contemporary English Tragedy*, London: University of Toronto Press, 2013, 231–84.

Chansky, Dorothy, *Composing Ourselves: The Little Theatre Movement and the American Audience*, Carbondale: Southern Illinois University Press, 2005.

Cole, Toby, ed., *Playwrights on Playwriting: The Meaning and Making of Modern Drama from Ibsen to Ionesco*, with introduction by John Gassner, London: MacGibbon and Kee, 1960.

Craig, Edward Gordon, *On the Art of the Theatre*, Chicago: Brown's Bookstore, 1911.

Crow, Brian and Chris Banfield, *An Introduction to Post-Colonial Theatre*, Cambridge: Cambridge University Press, 1996.

Deak, Frantisek, *Symbolist Theater: The Formation of an Avant-Garde*, Baltimore, MD: Johns Hopkins University Press, 1993.

Diamond, Elin, *Unmaking Mimesis*, London and New York: Routledge, 1997.

Eltis, Sos, *Revising Wilde: Society and Subversion in the Plays of Oscar Wilde*, Oxford: Oxford University Press, 1996.

Eltis, Sos, *Acts of Desire: Women and Sex on Stage 1800–1930*, Oxford: Oxford University Press, 2013.

Eltis, Sos and Kirsten E. Shepherd-Barr, 'What Was the New Drama?' in *Twenty-First Century Approaches to Literature: Victorian into Modern*, ed. Laura Marcus, Michèle Mendelssohn, and Kirsten Shepherd-Barr, Oxford: Oxford University Press, 2016.

Esslin, Martin, '"Dead! And never called me Mother!": The Missing Dimension in American Drama', *Studies in the Literary Imagination* (Fall 1988), 23–33.

Feldman, Alexander, *Dramas of the Past on the Twentieth-Century Stage*, London: Routledge, 2013.

Fuchs, Elinor, *The Death of Character: Perspectives on Theater after Modernism*, Bloomington: Indiana University Press, 1996.

Gilbert, Helen, and Joanne Tompkins, *Post-Colonial Drama: Theory, Practice, Politics*, London: Routledge, 1996.

Grene, Nicholas, *The Politics of Irish Drama: Plays in Context from Boucicault to Friel*, Cambridge: Cambridge University Press, 1999.

Grotowski, Jerzy, *Towards a Poor Theatre*, London: Simon and Schuster, 1969.

Hammond, Will and Dan Steward, eds, *Verbatim Verbatim: Contemporary Documentary Theatre*, London: Oberon, 2008.

Holledge, Julie, *Innocent Flowers: Women in the Edwardian Theatre*, London: Virago, 1981.

Innes, Christopher, *Avant-Garde Theatre, 1892–1992*, New York: Routledge, 1993.

Innes, Christopher, *Modern British Drama: The Twentieth Century*, 2nd edition, Cambridge: Cambridge University Press, 2002.

Kelly, Katherine E., *Modern Drama by Women 1880s–1930s: An International Anthology*, London: Routledge, 1996.

Kershaw, Baz, *The Radical in Performance: Between Brecht and Baudrillard*, London: Routledge, 1999.

Lehmann, Hans-Thies, *Postdramatic Theatre*, trans. Karen Jürs-Munby, London: Routledge, 2006.

Londré, Felicia Hardison and Daniel J. Watermeier, *The History of the North American Theater*, New York: Continuum, 2000.

McGrath, John, *A Good Night Out: Popular Theatre, Audience, Class, and Form*, London: Nick Hern Books, 1996.

McGuinness, Patrick, *Maurice Maeterlinck and the Making of Modern Theatre*, Oxford: Oxford University Press, 2000.

Megson, Chris, *Modern British Playwriting: The 1970s*, London: Bloomsbury, 2012.

Milling, Jane, ed., *Modern British Playwriting: The 1980s*, London: Bloomsbury, 2012.

Moi, Toril, *Henrik Ibsen and the Birth of Modernism*, Oxford: Oxford University Press, 2006.

Nicholson, Steve, *The Censorship of British Drama*, 3 vols, Exeter: University of Exeter Press, 2003–2011.

Nicholson, Steve, *Modern British Playwriting: The 1960s*, London: Bloomsbury, 2012.

Pattie, David, *Modern British Playwriting: The 1950s*, London: Bloomsbury, 2012.

Puchner, Martin, *Stage Fright: Modernism, Anti-Theatricality, and Drama*, Baltimore, MD: Johns Hopkins University Press, 2011 paperback.

Rebellato, Dan, *1956 and All That: The Making of Modern British Drama*, London: Routledge, 1999.

Rebellato, Dan, ed., *Modern British Playwriting: 2000–2009*, London: Bloomsbury, 2013.

Reinelt, Janelle, *After Brecht: British Epic Theatre*, Ann Arbor: University of Michigan Press, 1996.

Roach, Joseph R., 'Darwin's Passion: The Language of Expression on Nature's Stage', *Discourse* 13 (Fall/Winter 1990–1), 40–57.

Roose-Evans, James, *Experimental Theatre from Stanislavsky to Peter Brook*, New York: Routledge, 1996.

Rubin, Don, ed., *World Encyclopedia of Contemporary Theatre*, 5 vols, New York: Routledge, 1995–9.

Schumacher, Claude, ed., *Naturalism and Symbolism in European Theatre 1850–1918*, Cambridge: Cambridge University Press, 1995.

Shepherd-Barr, Kirsten, *Ibsen and Early Modernist Theatre, 1890–1900*, Westport, CT: Greenwood, 1997.

Shepherd-Barr, Kirsten, 'Staging Modernism', in *The Oxford Handbook of Modernisms*, ed. Peter Brooker, Andrzej Gasiorek, Deborah Longworth, and Andrew Thacker, Oxford: Oxford University Press, 2010.

Shepherd-Barr, Kirsten, *Science on Stage: From Doctor Faustus to Copenhagen*, Princeton, NJ: Princeton University Press, 2006; paperback 2012.

Shepherd-Barr, Kirsten, *Theatre and Evolution from Ibsen to Beckett*, New York: Columbia University Press, 2015.

Sierz, Aleks, *In-Yer-Face Theatre: British Drama Today*, London: Faber, 2001.

Sierz, Aleks, *Rewriting the Nation: British Theatre Today*, London: Methuen, 2011.

Sierz, Aleks, *Modern British Playwriting: The 1990s*, London: Bloomsbury, 2014.

Taxidou, Olga, 'Actors and Puppets: From Henry Irving's Lyceum to Edward Gordon Craig's Arena Goldoni' in *Twenty-First Century Approaches to Literature: Victorian into Modern*, ed. Laura Marcus, Michèle Mendelssohn, and Kirsten Shepherd-Barr, Oxford: Oxford University Press, 2016.

Watt, Stephen and Gary A. Richardson, *American Drama: Colonial to Contemporary*, Fort Worth, TX: Harcourt Brace, 1995.

Whyman, Rose, *Anton Chekhov*, London: Routledge, 2011.

Whyman, Rose, *The Stanislavsky System of Acting: Legacy and Influence in Modern Performance*, Cambridge: Cambridge University Press, 2011.

Wilmer, S.E., ed., *National Theatres in a Changing Europe*, London: Palgrave Macmillan, 2008.

Wilmeth, Don B. and Tice L. Miller, eds, *Cambridge Guide to American Theatre*, 2nd edition, New York: Cambridge University Press, 1996.

Witt, Mary Ann Frese, *Metatheater and Modernity: Baroque and Neobaroque*, Madison, NJ: Fairleigh Dickinson University Press, 2013.

Worthen, W.B., *Modern Drama: Plays, Criticism, Theory*, Boston: Harcourt Brace, 1995.

Publisher's acknowledgements

We are grateful for permission to include the following copyright material in this book.

Brecht's chart of Dramatic form of theatre vs Epic form of theatre © Marc Silberman, Steve Giles, and Tom Kuhn (eds), 2014, *Brecht on Theatre*, Methuen Drama, an imprint of Bloomsbury Publishing Plc.

The publisher and author have made every effort to trace and contact all copyright holders before publication. If notified, the publisher will be pleased to rectify any errors or omissions at the earliest opportunity.

Index

Index

ONLINE CATALOGUE
A Very Short Introduction

Our online catalogue is designed to make it easy to find your ideal Very Short Introduction. View the entire collection by subject area, watch author videos, read sample chapters, and download reading guides.

http://global.oup.com/uk/academic/general/vsi_list/

SOCIAL MEDIA
Very Short Introduction

Join our community

www.oup.com/vsi

- Join us online at the official Very Short Introductions **Facebook** page.
- Access the thoughts and musings of our authors with our online **blog**.
- Sign up for our monthly **e-newsletter** to receive information on all new titles publishing that month.
- Browse the full range of Very Short Introductions online.
- Read **extracts** from the Introductions for free.
- Visit our library of **Reading Guides**. These guides, written by our expert authors will help you to question again, why you think what you think.
- If you are a teacher or lecturer you can order inspection copies quickly and simply via our website.